# The New Baby Survival Guide for Men

## The All-in-One Handbook With Tricks and Hacks to The Baby's First Year For New Dads and First-Time Fathers

**Rocky Hunter**

© **Copyright 2023 - All rights reserved.**

The content contained within this book may not be reproduced, duplicated or transmitted without direct written permission from the author or the publisher.

Under no circumstances will any blame or legal responsibility be held against the publisher, or author, for any damages, reparation, or monetary loss due to the information contained within this book, either directly or indirectly.

Legal Notice:

This book is copyright protected. It is only for personal use. You cannot amend, distribute, sell, use, quote or paraphrase any part, or the content within this book, without the consent of the author or publisher.

Disclaimer Notice:

Please note the information contained within this document is for educational and entertainment purposes only. All effort has been executed to present accurate, up to date, reliable, complete information. No warranties of any kind are declared or implied. Readers acknowledge that the author is not engaged in the rendering of legal, financial, medical or professional advice. The content within this book has been derived from various sources. Please consult a licensed professional before attempting any techniques outlined in this book.

By reading this document, the reader agrees that under no circumstances is the author responsible for any losses, direct or indirect, that are incurred as a result of the use of the information contained within this document, including, but not limited to, errors, omissions, or inaccuracies.

# Table of Contents

**INTRODUCTION** .................................................................................. 1

**CHAPTER 1: WELCOME TO THE FIRST DAY OF YOUR BABY'S LIFE!** ......... 3

   EVERYTHING YOU NEED TO KNOW ABOUT THE FIRST DAY WITH YOUR BABY AND YOUR PARTNER .................................................................................. 3
      *Get Ready Dad, The Baby is Here!* ................................................. 4
      *Birth Defects You Should Keep an Eye Out For* .............................. 9
      *Taking Care of Your Partner After Childbirth* ................................ 22
      *Postpartum Depression* ................................................................ 26
      *Taking Care of Your Newborn* ....................................................... 32
      *Segue* ............................................................................................... 38

**CHAPTER 2: CUTE LITTLE FISTS AND CUTE LITTLE SOCKS** ................... 39

   EVERYTHING YOU NEED TO KNOW ABOUT THE DEVELOPMENT OF YOUR BABY OVER THE NEXT TWO MONTHS .................................................................... 39
      *Milestones and Changes in Your Baby During Month One* ........... 40
      *Milestones and Changes of a Baby During Month Two* ................ 48
      *Your Roles and Responsibilities as a Working Dad* ...................... 52
      *Segue* ............................................................................................... 56

**CHAPTER 3: SMILING BABIES, SLEEPLESS DADS!** ................................ 57

   FINDING BALANCE IN YOUR HOME AND WORK LIFE WHILE YOUR BABY CONTINUES DEVELOPING ..................................................................................... 57
      *Milestones and Changes in Your Baby at Three Months* .............. 58
      *Milestones and Changes in Your Baby at Four Months* ................ 62
      *Balancing Work and Baby as a New Dad* ..................................... 66
      *Segue* ............................................................................................... 71

**CHAPTER 4: BONDING WITH YOUR BABBLING BABY** ......................... 73

   DADS NEED TO BOND TOO! ................................................................ 73
      *Milestones and Changes in Your Baby at Five Months* ................ 73
      *Milestones and Changes in Your Baby at Six Months* .................. 77
      *Bonding With Your Baby* ............................................................... 80
      *Segue* ............................................................................................... 84

**CHAPTER 5: THE TEETHING BABY AND A SEETHING YOU** ............... 85

   ADJUSTING TO LIFE WITH A TEETHING BABY! ............................................. 85
      *Milestones and Changes in Your Baby at Seven Months* ............ 86
      *Milestones and Changes in Your Baby at Eight Months* ............. 89
      *How to Help Your Partner Embrace Their Role as a New Mom* ..... 92
      *Self-Care Strategies For New Dads* ............................................. 95
      *Segue* ............................................................................................ 99

**CHAPTER 6: THE CAUTIOUS DAD OF A MOVING BABY** ................... 101

   FROM CRAWLING TO WALKING...AND SO MUCH MORE! ............................. 101
      *Milestones and Changes in Your Baby During Months Nine to Ten* ............................................................................................ 102
      *Milestones and Changes in Your Baby During Months 11 & 12* ... 105
      *Emotional, Social, and Mental Development of Babies and What You Can Do as a Dad* ................................................................... 109
      *Segue* .......................................................................................... 112

**APPENDICES** ........................................................................... 113

   BABY FEEDING CHART ........................................................................ 113
   VACCINATION CHART ......................................................................... 114
   BABY MILESTONE CHART (1-12 MONTHS) ............................................ 116

**CONCLUSION** .......................................................................... 119

**REFERENCES** ........................................................................... 121

Thanks for purchasing my book. After you have finished reading the book, I would really appreciate it if you could help spread the word and leave a review on Amazon so we can reach a greater audience and help them in the same way that we have hopefully helped you. To leave a review, scan the QR code below with your mobile phone and click on the book. Once you have clicked on the book, you will be able to find the button to leave a review. If you do not own a smartphone, please search for my book on Amazon and take 60 seconds to leave a review. You are amazing!

# Introduction

*Anyone who tells you fatherhood is the greatest thing that can happen to you, they are understanding it.* –Mike Myers

Fatherhood is a remarkable journey that a man embarks on when he first learns that his partner is pregnant. There is no greater joy than finding out you have been blessed with the title "Dad"! Even though you are well aware of the fact that it's going to be a long, tiring journey, you can't help but scream and jump for joy because of the instant love you already have for your baby. Coming to terms with being a father, and understanding that you now have a role to fulfill takes a level of maturity that a lot of men don't have nowadays. People have their own perspectives of what it means to be a father, and not everyone shares the same understanding when it comes to fatherhood. However, the core definition of a father, which every culture can identify with, is someone who is there to protect, provide, and teach their child right from wrong.

A father is someone you can turn to whenever you find yourself in deep trouble. He is someone who loves in his own way and will go above and beyond to give you whatever you need, even if it means he has to make a few sacrifices in the process. He is charming, compassionate, and caring, but he can also turn into a disciplinarian when the need arises. Sounds like a lot, yeah? You're probably thinking, how on earth can a man have all those different qualities at the same time, and most of these characteristics you probably don't even recognize in yourself right now! It's scary, I agree, but it doesn't mean that you cannot develop all these traits within yourself as time goes by. Fatherhood comes naturally, so don't overthink it.

Consider this, the positive pregnancy test has given you a headstart so that you could get used to the idea of becoming a father. But if you haven't built up your confidence yet, there must be a reason behind that. Most first-time dads hold themselves back because they have an extreme fear of not knowing what to do with a newborn baby. This fear keeps them from spending time bonding with their baby, and the only way they can overcome this fear is by conquering it with knowledge! What do people do when they don't know something? They google it, seek advice from friends and family, or they buy a book to help them gain some insight into the topic. You have chosen to seek advice and guidance from this book, so get ready to become the best dad you could ever be! This amazing guide will teach you everything you need to know about taking care of your newborn baby.

Remember dads, everyone's journey is different. Don't compare your experience of fatherhood to anyone else's. Make this journey your own by focusing on your own strengths and weaknesses as a first-time dad. You will make mistakes, and you will learn from them. Eventually, you will develop your own parenting style that is tailored to your newborn. This is what's good for your baby—a father who will mold himself into the dad that his children need. Open your heart, and prepare your mind. Let all fear melt away, because it will only hinder your learning. Embrace an attitude of positivity, and believe in yourself. God would have never blessed you with the responsibility of fatherhood if he knew that you were going to mess things up! So have faith in yourself, dad. By the time you have finished reading this book, you will be overflowing with confidence and excitement to embrace your role as a father. Get ready! Your journey into fatherhood begins right now!

# Chapter 1:

## Welcome to the First Day of Your Baby's Life!

*When you hold your baby in your arms the first time, and you think of all the things you can say and do to influence him, it's a tremendous responsibility. What you do with him can influence not only him, but everyone he meets, and not for a day or a month or a year, but for time and eternity.* –Rose Kennedy

## Everything You Need to Know About the First Day With Your Baby and Your Partner

In this chapter, you are going to learn the important aspects of taking care of a newborn and helping your partner after delivery. This can be a very exciting, yet nerve-racking, time for dads because reality finally hits them. Everything you need to know about a newborn's health, what to look out for, how to take care of your partner and be there for her, and how to look after an infant, is highlighted in this chapter. Once you develop an understanding of what needs to be taken care of on the first day, you will no longer stress about it—in fact, you will be excited!

## *Get Ready Dad, The Baby is Here!*

Welcome to the first day of your life with a newborn! Quite exciting, right? Since the day you first heard that your partner was expecting, you've been eagerly waiting to meet your little angel. You and your partner must have talked about the things you would say to your baby, which outfit to put on first, and who would be on diaper duty on the first night. Well, that incredible moment has finally come! But now that your baby is here, do you have what it takes to make sure that you are looking after them well? First-time dads are terrified of holding their newborns, and it typically has to do with the fact that they don't understand how to cradle a baby correctly. A lack of knowledge introduces an intense fear which is housed within the mind. The key to breaking this fear lies in educating yourself with as much knowledge as possible. Taking care of your partner and a newborn is a lot of responsibility, especially when you are dealing with your own mixed emotions of joy, excitement, fear, and uncertainty. While dad is taking care of mom and baby, who is going to take care of dad? It can be overwhelming for a first-time dad to handle all of this responsibility so fast, but there's no doubt that you can do it perfectly. It's important to have a strong support system around you during this time. Planning can help you a great deal, but only if you know how to plan and what to plan for. This chapter will help you prepare yourself for the arrival of your baby, and we aren't just talking about packing the hospital bag. There are many other exciting aspects to cover. Let's start off by exploring what happens on the day that your baby is born. There is quite a long list of things to talk about, so brace yourself for a journey of learning dad!

## *So, What Does a Newborn Look Like?*

Ahh, the vision of a cute, plumpy cherub-looking baby probably crosses your mind every time you think about what your newborn would look like as soon as they make their exit from the womb. Well, you're in for a surprise dad! Your newborn will be covered by all kinds of bodily fluids—both mom's and baby's—which play a role in making the delivery much easier. These fluids—the amniotic and vernix—were present in the womb with your baby, and they helped develop your baby's taste and smell senses. Straight after the doctor delivers the baby, their body color might be a bit blue or pale and whitish because of the amniotic fluid, but soon, it will return to normal. It usually turns pink within a few minutes after birth. One of the first things you might notice is the shape of your baby's head. It might look slightly pointed at the top because of passing through the birth canal during vaginal delivery. Don't worry though, this alien look is temporary. After a few days, your baby's head will take on a normal, well-rounded shape. Some babies are even born with a beautiful head of hair! It's believed that moms who ate a lot of green vegetables during pregnancy, will give birth to a baby who has a lot of hair.

Babies usually return to their fetal position shortly after birth, with their fists closed tightly and held against their chest, and their legs bent upwards towards their stomach. They will remain in this snuggled-up position for a few days, and their limbs will stretch out gradually with time. Your baby's hands and legs look so tiny and fragile, and their paper-thin nails on their fingers are extremely sharp, so they might scratch up their face within the first few days. When you look at your baby's face, you might notice a scrunched-up forehead which makes your baby look all fussed up and grumpy. These lines will smoothen out within a few days. Your baby will only take on their cherub-like features after a few weeks when fat fills under their skin and plumps them out.

## Baby's First 24-Hours

Soon after your baby is born, doctors and nurses will begin performing an array of tests to make sure that they are healthy. The first 24 hours are crucial because it reveals a lot about any hidden illnesses that your baby might have which didn't show up on the ultrasound scans. These first few hours are also important for you and your partner, as parents use this time to bond with their babies. Let's take a look at what happens in the first 24 hours so you can get a better understanding of what to expect as a new father.

## The First Five Minutes After Delivery

As soon as your baby is born, the doctor will have to suction out the baby's nose and mouth to remove the amniotic fluid and mucus that has been trapped in the airway. Once the mucus has been cleared up, your baby will begin breathing normally. Next, the umbilical cord will need to be clamped and cut, and most of the time the honor is given to the fathers to do this so brace yourself, dad, this is no time to be passing out! After this is done, the doctors can start working on determining your baby's heart rate, reflex response, color, breathing, and muscle tone one minute after delivery, and then again five minutes after delivery. This is known as the Apgar score, and scores usually range between zero and ten. In order for a baby to be considered healthy, they must get a score above seven.

Most babies score an eight or nine, however, if your baby's score is lower than seven, it could indicate that something is wrong, but no need to get worked up just yet because most babies who have a lower score at birth tend to have the test redone at regular intervals, and their score increases eventually. There should only be a real cause for concern if your baby's score doesn't pick up at all, especially after having the tests redone numerous times. Once the tests are complete, the nurses will wipe down your baby and remove all the excess fluids and blood from their body. Now your newborn looks more like a baby and less like an alien. Next, the nurses will place your baby in a warmer until they are able to regulate and maintain their own body temperature naturally.

## *Hour One*

While you and your partner are still in the delivery room, the doctor will administer a Vitamin K injection to your baby, preferably on the thigh, to help prevent any clotting problems that might occur after birth. The nurse will also rub some antibiotic eye ointment onto your baby's eyes to prevent any infection that could arise from passing through the birth canal. If your baby was born prematurely (before 40 weeks), then the doctor will transfer the baby to the neonatal ICU for monitoring. Breastfeeding is encouraged within the first hour of delivery, so assist your partner with the first feeding. However, if your baby is premature, the bonding experience will be delayed until your baby is no longer at risk for infection. Premie babies are at high risk for developing infections because their immune systems are still developing. This means that they can get sick easily. Nevertheless, if you have a healthy full-term baby, they will be transferred with the mother to the recovery room.

## *Hours Two to Three*

Now that your partner and your baby are in the recovery room, you can help her begin the breastfeeding journey. This might take some time, especially for the baby to latch onto the breast, and your partner will be exhausted and in pain by now. Whether she has had a c-section or vaginal delivery, it will be difficult for her during this first hour. Be there to support her in every way that you can. Within the second or third hour, the nurse will come into the recovery room to check on the mother and the baby. She will check your baby's pulse, examine the abdomen, and confirm that your baby has ten fingers and ten toes. The nurse will also inspect the baby's genitals to make sure that it has developed properly. Then she will record something called the Ballard Score, which involves examining the length of your baby, and making sure that the circumference of their head and the circumference of their chest are the right measurements according to their gestational age. If your baby is premature, she will remain in the NICU where her vitals will be closely monitored and checked regularly—once every 30 minutes within the first two hours.

## Hours Four Through 22

This is when you will have more time to bond with your baby, along with your partner. You can assist the nurse when she gives your baby their very first bath. I know this might sound a bit scary, but don't worry because the nurse will be holding your baby. Your baby might also pass their first stool during this time, which is called meconium, so get ready to change your very first diaper dad! The color of the stool will be dark brown or black, so don't be alarmed—this is entirely normal. Your partner will also be included in these bonding moments, so you can do things together as a team for your baby. The nurse will teach you how to swaddle your newborn with a receiver blanket once the bath is over.

Swaddling is an important technique because it helps keep your baby wrapped up in the same position they were in, in the womb. When babies are swaddled properly, they feel secure and warm, so they are less likely to become restless. If your partner wants to breastfeed exclusively, there will be a lactation consultant who will come in during this time to help your partner learn more about breastfeeding. Some women have enough milk in their breasts by the time they deliver, so feeding won't be too much of a hassle. However, there are some women who have to wait a day or two for their milk to come in. The more the baby suckles at the breast, the quicker the milk will come in.

## *Hours 23 and 24*

Time for more tests for your little one! I know that it might seem like there are so many tests being done, but rest assured that each of these tests are extremely important for your baby. The doctor will come in to conduct an examination of your baby to determine if they are feeding and resting well. A test for jaundice will be conducted as well because newborn babies are at high risk of developing a condition called yellow jaundice. This occurs when the baby's liver cannot break down bilirubin, and this causes their skin and eyes to turn yellow in color. If left untreated, jaundice can lead to brain damage, so doctors place these babies under a special light that helps break down the bilirubin. Hereafter, the doctor will prick your baby's heel to run more tests which can only be conducted during this stage. After 24 hours, a baby's blood levels rise once they start feeding regularly which makes it the perfect time to conduct these tests which check for 50 different types of metabolic diseases.

## *Birth Defects You Should Keep an Eye Out For*

A birth defect is something that isn't normal with your newborn baby. It could be a physical anomaly that you can see on your baby's body, or it could be a chemical anomaly that has occurred within the baby's brain, or there could be an internal anomaly with your baby's organs. Although many defects can be predicted using ultrasound, and various other tests taken during the course of pregnancy, some defects are found much later on. Birth defects can interfere with a child's ability to walk, talk, and even eat. This takes a huge toll on the parents who have to work extra hard to help their children do the basic everyday functions. This is terrifying for all parents to think about, and some can compose themselves enough to stay calm when they meet their baby for the first time because they have been made aware of their baby's abnormalities during pregnancy by a doctor or nurse when a scan was conducted. However, for those parents who are caught by surprise when their babies are born, it can be difficult to come to terms with the diagnosis. Parents can make themselves more aware of the signs that could indicate their baby might have a birth defect. It's always better to have a good understanding of these things so you can be more involved in your baby's diagnosis.

## *How Are Birth Defects Caused?*

There are several causes for birth defects in newborn babies, however, it can be a challenge to determine what exactly caused a birth defect in a particular baby without having enough information about the parents and their health history. Since birth defects have become more common over the years, there have been numerous studies carried out to understand how these birth defects develop in certain babies. Here are a few reasons why babies are born with some kind of abnormality.

## *Genetic Abnormalities*

A small percentage of all birth defects are caused by some sort of genetic disorder. Abnormalities such as down syndrome and cystic fibrosis are caused by a chromosomal malfunction that arises from a genetic abnormality. Another key reason why babies are born with genetic abnormalities is that both parents are related by blood (consanguinity). For instance, a brother and a sister conceived a baby together. Because of this blood relation, this baby can be born with some type of disorder. Also, if either of the parents has a pre-existing disorder themselves, such as down syndrome or Autism, there is a high chance it could be passed from parent to child through their DNA.

## *Malnutrition and Poor Access to Basic Healthcare*

Unfortunately, birth defects are most common in low-income areas, such as India and Africa, where parents have no access to proper healthcare. This means that pregnant women have no multivitamins such as folic acid and iron tablets to take during their pregnancy. Living in low-income areas also means that there is usually a shortage of food. People eat once every three or four days, depending on their ability to find good food to eat. Otherwise, they survive on oatmeal and bread most of the time, which isn't good enough for pregnant women because they need nutrients to grow a healthy baby. Without proper nourishment, these women are forced to give birth to babies that are underweight and born with certain birth defects. Malnourishment can also occur in high-income areas, where women suffer from extreme nausea and vomiting during pregnancy (hyperemesis gravidarum). As a result of this illness, they cannot keep any food in their stomach long enough for their babies to benefit. This sickness usually dies off by month three of pregnancy, however, some women suffer throughout.

## *Drug and Alcohol Use*

Women who use drugs and alcohol during pregnancy put their babies at a high risk for developing brain deformities, among many other birth defects. When babies have been exposed to alcohol and drug addiction during pregnancy, they are born with withdrawal symptoms which most babies can't survive for long. Because drugs and alcohol alter the brain chemistry, it causes a lot of memory loss and intellectual disability in the person who is taking them. When a woman is pregnant, she passes these chemicals onto her baby via her blood. Can you imagine what these chemicals do to a baby's brain that is still developing? It slows down the developmental process and causes abnormalities to occur. As a result, babies are born with all kinds of brain disorders which affect their ability to have a normal life.

## *Different Types of Birth Defects and the Signs*

Birth defects can be classified into the following categories: structural defects, functional and developmental defects. Structural defects are deformities that develop on the physical body which are visible. For instance, when a body part is malformed or missing completely from the body. This includes the organs inside the body as well. Functional and developmental defects are deformities that occur due to developmental problems in the brain or in the body's system. Let's take a closer look at the various types of birth defects and how you can identify them.

## *Structural Defects*

### Heart defects

Also known as congenital heart disease, a heart defect can occur in the walls of the heart, in the valves, or in the blood vessels. There are several types of congenital heart defects, and they all range in severity. Some defects aren't severe enough, so they don't display any noticeable signs. Others are serious enough to threaten the lives of these babies. The signs of heart defects in newborns include:

- a blue color in the fingers, toes, skin, and lips
- shortness of breath or trouble breathing
- the baby doesn't feed properly
- born with a low weight
- pain in the chest
- delayed growth

### Cleft Lip or Cleft Palate

When a baby is born with a split or a cut on their lip, it is known as a cleft lip, and when a baby's mouth cannot close properly because of poor development during pregnancy, it is known as a cleft palate. The exact cause of this deformity is unknown; however, doctors and scientists believe that it can be caused by genetics, drinking and smoking during pregnancy, or not taking prenatal vitamins such as folic acid which is essential for fetal development. The signs of a cleft lip or a cleft palate are as follows:

- The first sign is a cut on the upper lip of your baby's mouth.

- When you feed your baby, milk might come running out of their nose because the barrier between the nose and the mouth has not developed.

- Frequent ear infections.

- Speech impairment.

**Clubfoot**

Clubfoot is a common birth defect that causes a baby's foot to turn inwards instead of outwards. This abnormality can be picked up on an ultrasound scan during pregnancy. This condition usually only affects one foot, but there have been cases where both feet are affected. Although the exact cause is unknown, it is believed by doctors that it can be passed down from parent to child, if there has been a history of clubfoot originating from that particular parent. Also, if the mother smokes and drinks alcohol during pregnancy, it increases the risk of the baby being born with these deformities. This abnormality can be corrected with the help of physical therapy and a training brace which the baby will be required to wear on their feet.

## Functional and Developmental Defects

### Down Syndrome

Down syndrome is a common birth defect by which a baby is born with an extra set of 21st chromosomes. This birth defect is also known as trisomy 21. When a child has Down syndrome, they experience significant delays in their mental and physical development. There is no cure for Down syndrome; however, there is hope for living a normal life, even though the life expectancy is short. The signs of down syndrome are as follows:

- Facial features look flat and oddly shaped.
- The baby's neck will be short.
- No healthy muscle tone.
- Head and ears are smaller.
- A bulging tongue
- Eyes slant upwards.

### Sickle Cell Disease

This is a birth defect that occurs inside the body. It is a genetic disease of the red blood cells. Normal red blood cells are disc-shaped, and they pass through the blood vessels easily. However, babies with sickle cell disease have red blood cells that are shaped like a sickle. This makes it difficult to pass through blood vessels, causing these cells to become trapped in certain vessels.

This can be very painful and may lead to tissue damage. This condition is prevalent in countries such as India, Africa, Saudi Arabia, and the Mediterranean. Babies who are born with Sickle cell disease, have to live with this condition for the rest of their lives. The symptoms are as follows:

- Jaundice in newborn babies.
- Fussiness and irritability.
- Significant swelling in the baby's hands and feet.
- Pain in the baby's chest, back, legs, and arms.

**Cystic Fibrosis**

(CF) Cystic fibrosis is a condition that causes severe damage to the respiratory system, as well as to the digestive system. This is a genetic disorder that is passed onto the baby by the parents, and there is no cure for it. CF can be managed with certain medications and treatments. The organs that are most severely affected are the lungs, liver, pancreas, and the intestines. Babies who have CF are very troublesome and restless. Here's what to look out for in babies who might have CF.

- A strong salty taste to the baby's skin, which is noticed when parents kiss their baby.
- Respiratory problems such as wheezing, coughing, recurrent chest infections, and sinus issues.
- Digestive issues such as foul-smelling stool, inability to gain weight, nausea, swollen abdomen, and loss of appetite.
- Delayed growth in children.

## How to Cope After Hearing That Your Child Has a Birth Defect

Hearing that your baby has a birth defect is the worst news any parent could get. At that moment, it would seem like all the dreams you had envisioned for your child are being crushed in front of you and there is nothing you can do about it. Feelings of helplessness and grief engulf you, and all you can think about is how to pick yourself up so you can be the best parent to your newborn baby. You will experience denial at first, which will make it very difficult to keep your sanity. But once that phase passes, and you are forced to face reality, there are some key points you should remember to help you find your way again, so you can be the parent your child needs.

### Don't Blame Yourself

Blaming yourself, or your partner, for the diagnosis of your baby's condition, isn't going to make things better. Most birth defects happen for reasons that are out of your control as a parent. If you and your partner did everything you could to ensure that you were taking the necessary precautions for a healthy pregnancy, then you shouldn't be blaming yourselves for anything. When you blame yourself, or your partner, for something you had no control over, it causes you to lose focus on your baby. Try to keep your emotions in check, and pay attention to the matter at hand. Your focus should be on how to help your baby now.

### You Are Not Alone

Parents who receive the news that their child has been born with a birth defect, often feel alone and isolated from everyone else, especially if they are the first ones in their family to have children born with some sort of condition. You are not alone.

There are thousands of parents out there who had to hear the same news you did. Don't feel like God singled you out. Reach out to other parents who are going through the same experience as you. There are support groups online, and classes for parents who want to learn how to take care of their special needs babies.

## Find a Medical Team You Can Trust

It's normal to feel protective over your baby, especially after finding out that they have a birth defect. Finding the right team of doctors and nurses is extremely important, so you should start working on that. Once you are confident that your baby is in good hands, it will take a huge weight off your shoulders. Every parent wants their special needs child to have the best care possible because it would mean that their child's pain and discomfort are being managed well.

## Take Care of Yourself, and Your Partner

Taking care of a baby with a birth defect is no easy task. Parents have to be extra careful when it comes to feeding, bathing, and dressing their babies. This requires a lot of time and energy, which means that parents will become drained out very quickly. It's crucial that you look after yourself if you want your baby to be in good hands. Eat on time, take a bath, and rest when you can. Share the workload between you and your partner, and take turns watching the baby. If you need an extra pair of hands, consider hiring a nanny with training in taking care of special needs babies. Don't take on more than you can handle, because a tired mom or dad can't give their baby their best.

## *NICU and Emotionally Helping Your Partner*

When babies are born prematurely, or if there is a problem with their health, they are moved to the NICU (Neonatal Intensive Unit). These babies are watched around the clock by specialist doctors and nurses who can provide them with the care they need. Some babies stay in the NICU for a few hours, whilst others remain there for months until they are healthy enough to be sent home with their parents. Babies who are born prematurely (before seven months), have to stay in the NICU until they are fully developed. Other babies, with birth defects and other health concerns, remain in the NICU until they have received the proper treatment and are healthy enough. Parents can visit the NICU at any time, but visitors aren't allowed in. The only exception would be for a religious leader such as a Pastor or healer to come in and pray for the baby.

### *Questions Parents Should Ask*

Here are some questions you should ask if your baby is sent to the NICU. It's good to understand what is happening and why, especially if your baby has a health condition. These questions will help you understand what is happening around you, so you won't have to feel stressed or anxious.

- Why is my baby in the NICU?
- How long will my baby have to stay here?
- Can I touch or hold my baby?
- Will I be able to stay with my baby in the NICU?
- What are the treatments that my baby is receiving?

- Can you tell me about the daily care plan you have set up?

- What are the side effects of the medications that my baby is taking?

- Can I breastfeed or bottle-feed my baby?

- What are some of the tests that will be done for my baby?

## How to Support Your Partner When Your Baby is in the NICU

Dads, it can be emotionally and physically exhausting for your partner during their stay in the NICU. Your wife is solely responsible for taking care of your baby during this time, especially if she is breastfeeding. Her motherly instincts will have her on edge throughout the day and night, and this can be really stressful. All she wants to do is comfort the baby, and make sure that she is doing everything she can to get your baby healthy and happy. There's no doubt that she will need your help and support during this time. Here's what you can do to be there for your partner while your baby is in the NICU.

- **Take Care of Your Partner**

Bring your partner something to eat from time to time, especially if she is breastfeeding. She will need her energy to take care of your baby, so make sure she eats and has plenty of water. Sleep is also very important, and women who have just given birth will need all the rest they can get. However, when moms are stressed, they find it hard to get some shut-eye. Reassure your partner, and encourage her to sleep whenever she can. Help her take a bath if she has trouble standing up (which is common for women who have had c-sections). Comb her hair if you can, and offer to massage her feet or back if she's experiencing any pain. Make sure she takes her medication as well if she has any health conditions of her own.

- **Communicate With Her**

If your partner is having a hard time emotionally, be there to talk with her about her feelings. Share your concerns with her as well, and don't hide your emotions either. It helps to know that you are also going through a difficult time, so she will feel like you can relate to her experience. Keeping the connection alive between you two is important. If you and your partner cannot communicate well, your relationship will suffer. You both need to be each other's support system, and the only way that is possible is if you talk to one another. After an exhausting day in the NICU, your partner will feel the urge to vent, to have her feelings heard. When she does, just be there to listen. Don't ignore her or downplay her feelings in any way. Try your best to understand.

- **Help With the Baby**

Offer to help your partner with the baby as much as you can. If she is bottle-feeding, offer to take the night shift so she can rest. Help her bathe the baby, change diapers, and make the baby sleep. Bonding time is also crucial for dads, just as much as it is for moms. Leaving your partner alone to take care of the baby because you are scared of holding the baby, or feeding the baby, will only put her at risk of becoming overwhelmed. This can worsen postpartum depression, so please try your best to help her in every way that you can.

## *Taking Care of Your Partner After Childbirth*

This section was discussed in detail in the last chapter of the previous book, so we will briefly mention a few key points. You would think that most dads are completely involved in taking care of their partners after childbirth, however, this isn't always the case. In countries like India, men have no responsibility when it comes to looking after their wives who have just given birth. They don't help their wives with their own care, nor do they help take care of the baby. Instead, the women are sent away to their maternal homes where their family is expected to nurse the mother back to health and take care of the newborn baby. In more developed countries such as America, dads have become more involved with helping their wives recover after birth, even if it means keeping the house tidy or cooking meals every day. Men have realized that childbirth is extremely difficult for women. They have finally understood their responsibilities extend to taking care of their newborn baby, as well as making sure that their wives are healing well and restoring their health. You can do the same for your partner by following the tips below. They will help you step into your new role as a new and improved husband and father.

**Create a New Normal**

Having a baby completely changes your life in ways you never thought were possible. Most parents envision their lives with their babies as a peaceful, playful time that brings joy and excitement into their daily routine. While this is very true, there is also another side to parenting that people don't talk about much. It's called the "new normal." Life after a baby is difficult to adjust to because people don't prepare themselves mentally or emotionally to deal with the challenges that they have to face. You can make things easier for yourself and for your partner by embracing the challenges that come with life after having a baby. Let go of the fantasy you envisioned for your life, and take each day as it comes. Things have changed, so don't place unrealistic expectations on one another. You both have a responsibility toward your baby, and toward each other, so try your best to adjust to this new life you have been blessed with.

## *Get Used to a Lack of Sleep*

Welcome to the world of no sleep for the next couple of months dad! Say bye to waking up late on Sunday mornings, and to laying in bed just lazing around until you muster up the energy to take a shower. Your baby has to adjust to life outside the womb, and this can take a while! Babies don't understand the difference between day and night, so they will wake up every two to three hours for a feed during the first two months. This means that you and your partner will have to wake up with your baby, which ultimately means less sleep for you both. This can be extremely frustrating, especially if you have to get up in the mornings for work every day. But if you prepare your mind early, you will be able to adjust. Less sleep for your partner also means that she will be cranky all the time. Once a baby completes three months, they will learn how to find a sleep routine which will help you a lot.

## *Keep An Eye On Her Mood*

Women become very moody after giving birth, and it's all thanks to those raging hormones. She will lash out at you and argue over little things. Her exhaustion will only make things worse, and her lack of "me time" will most definitely set her moods off at random times throughout the day. Women need time to themselves for self-care, and when they don't get this time, they can turn into monsters. Keep an eye on her moods, and try to figure out why she is feeling this way. Maybe she needs a nap, or maybe she wants a few minutes by herself. Don't fight back if she starts an argument with you. Try to understand that she is communicating her needs through her emotions. If she becomes too stressed out and emotionally exhausted, she could develop postpartum depression. We will discuss this further in the next section.

## *Be Good to Yourself and to Your Partner*

Don't forget to take care of yourself, dad. Your baby and your partner are relying on you to be the strong one in the family during this time. If you are not well physically or emotionally, you won't have anything to give to your family. As the famous saying goes, "You can't pour from an empty cup" so please take some time to rest, eat well, and do whatever you need to remove some stress from your mind. When you are healthy, you can help take care of your wife and baby. The same rule applies to your partner. If she isn't taken care of, her cup will also run dry. She needs to be healthy and well-rested so that she can be her best for the baby. Do whatever you can to help make her feel better about herself. Cook her a healthy meal, make her a cup of tea, or help her around the house. These little things mean a lot to women, especially when they cannot do these things themselves. Tell her how much you appreciate her, and reassure her that she is doing a great job.

## *Divide and Conquer*

The secret to a happy relationship is working together to get things done. Share the household responsibilities, take turns watching over the baby, and help one another get through the most stressful days. When you share the physical workload, as well as the emotional workload, you can get things done quicker, and no one has to feel overworked in the process. Offer help without your partner having to nag you for it all the time. If you see something that needs attention, take on that task and complete it. If you are tired, politely tell your partner that you need a few minutes to recharge, but you promise to get the task done. When it comes to taking care of the baby, rotate shifts every other day. The night shift shouldn't have to be just one person's responsibility. If you're a working dad, take on the night shifts twice a week, and again over the weekend. When two people work together, life becomes much easier.

## Be Patient When it Comes to Sex

Sex after childbirth is long desired by both parties—more so by the husband than the wife. It is the long wait to rekindle the intimacy between you and your partner which fuels your desire to jump at sex any chance you get. However, there is a reason why doctors say that a woman should wait up to six weeks before having sex. Delivering a baby takes a huge toll on a woman's body. Whether it was a natural vaginal birth or a c-section, the reproductive organs need time to heal and settle back into place—especially the womb. While the healing process is taking place, your partner might not feel the urge to engage in any type of sexual activity. Sometimes, it might take longer than six weeks for her to start feeling like herself again. So be patient and understanding when it comes to sex. Talk about other forms of sexual activity, and see how you both feel about it. Soon, your partner will be ready to get intimate with you, so don't rush the process. It will definitely be worth the wait!

## Postpartum Depression

The birth of a baby is a powerful experience that can trigger a number of different emotions in a woman. She might feel happy, sad, excited, and terrified all at the same time, and she probably wouldn't even realize it. Most moms experience postpartum depression just a few days after giving birth to their babies. It shows up suddenly, completely unannounced, and these women have no idea that they're dealing with postpartum depression. Some of them just chalk it down to being too tired, or being overstimulated by their newborns. This lack of identifying postpartum depression early on is what leads to it becoming worse over time. There have been cases where women have taken their own lives because they felt helpless in their depression. Understanding the signs and symptoms will help you detect it in your partner early on.

*Signs of Postpartum Depression*

Postpartum depression is a condition that is brought on by childbirth in women. It typically begins a few days after the baby is born, and it can last for months if not treated soon enough. Women who go through this type of depression, display certain signs that can prove to be helpful for getting help as soon as possible. Here's what you should keep an eye out for.

- Frequent mood swings that are difficult to control.
- Panic attacks and severe anxiety.
- Crying and feeling sad all the time (more than usual).
- Finding it hard to bond with the baby.
- Depressed and lacks excitement when she is around the baby.
- Withdrawing from everyone in the home.
- Always spending time alone.
- No appetite and refuses to eat food.
- Insomnia, or wanting to sleep all the time.
- No energy and feeling fatigued.
- Feeling like she isn't a good mom.

- Feeling guilty, worthless, and shameful for reasons unknown.

- Intense anger and easily irritated.

- Being paranoid with the baby.

- Might have thoughts about harming herself and the baby.

## How is Postpartum Depression Treated?

If you have noticed these signs in your partner, chances are that they have postpartum depression. However, it's important that she visits the doctor and gets a proper diagnosis. Sometimes, postpartum depression can be mistaken for another milder form of depression known as the "baby blues." This is a short phase that mothers go through after delivering their babies, and it only lasts a few weeks or so. Postpartum depression lasts much longer than a few weeks. Once your partner has been diagnosed, she will be treated by a healthcare professional in the following ways:

### Antidepressant Medications

- Selective serotonin reuptake inhibitors (SSRIs) such as Zoloft and Prozac.

- Serotonin norepinephrine reuptake inhibitors (SNRIs) such as Cymbalta and Pristiq.

- Wellbutrin or Zyban.

- Tricyclic antidepressants such as Elavil and Trophinal.

## Non-Medication Treatments

- Cognitive behavioral therapy
- Psychotherapy
- Calm breathing exercises
- Meditation

Women do recover from their postpartum depression, they just need extra care from their loved ones, and the love and support from their partners. As long as your wife is surrounded by a positive atmosphere, she will recover well. If the home is chaotic, and there are lots of fights and arguments, it will be harder for her to recover. Next, we take a look at how dads cope after the birth of their babies.

### *Do You Have Paternal Postnatal Depression?*

Believe it or not, fathers also go through depression after their babies are born. There have been studies conducted which show 1 in every 10 dads battle with postpartum anxiety and depression (Horsager-Boehrer). The reason why this has been overlooked for so many years is that men are often ignored when it comes to their mental health. As more and more dads began to come forward and share their experiences, there has been much light shed on this topic. Signs of paternal postnatal depression can set in before the baby even arrives, and in some cases, men have reported that they experienced depression months before their babies were born.

## *Signs of Paternal Postnatal Depression*

It can be difficult for dads to recognize signs of paternal postnatal depression in themselves, so consider asking a trusted friend or family member to help you with identifying the signs in yourself. Here's what you should be looking for.

- Lacking the drive and motivation to get anything done.
- Having angry outbursts that sometimes turn violent.
- Become more impulsive, and aren't afraid of taking risks.
- Turning to substances such as drugs and alcohol to ease your depression.
- Cannot concentrate at work or at home.
- Having suicidal thoughts.
- Withdrawing from family and friends.
- Spending more time at work to avoid coming home.
- Not spending enough time with the baby.

If you think that you might be experiencing postnatal depression, consider visiting the doctor and get diagnosed properly. Your mental health is just as important as mom's, so get yourself the help you need to be 100% healthy for your family and for yourself. Treatment works the same way as it does for moms who have postpartum depression.

## Ways You Can Help Your Partner With Postpartum Depression

Your role as a husband is more paramount than you think it is, especially when it comes to being that rock of support for your partner. There is so much you can do to help make things easier for your partner through her depression. She might not recognize your efforts just yet, but she will definitely be grateful to you once she recovers. If you don't know where to start, or what to do, follow the tips given below to get started. From then on out, taking care of your partner will become second nature to you.

### Be There Emotionally, Just as You Are Physically

Men often get so caught up with their jobs, and with helping out around the house, that they completely forget to make themselves emotionally available to connect with their partners. When your wife is going through postpartum depression, remind yourself to open up emotionally, and make yourself available for her when she needs to talk or vent about her feelings. Try not to dismiss her emotions, or her concerns, no matter how unrealistic they might seem—to her, they are very real. Tell her how much you love her, and remind her that she is going to get through this soon. Joke with her and make her laugh, and cry with her when she feels depressed. The only way she is going to get over her depression is by going through it first.

### Take Up Some of the Household Chores

As mentioned previously, helping out around the house is a great way to support your partner through postpartum depression. Waking up to an untidy home, and realizing that there isn't any food in the house, are all triggers that can set off depressive episodes. The last thing your partner needs is to feel as if she is incapable. You can wash the dishes after supper dad, and take out the trash every night. Cook supper a few times a week if you can, and help neaten up the home whenever necessary. Working as a team and getting things done together is great for restoring balance to your life.

## Encourage Your Partner to Spend Time With Friends or to Do Something She Loves

Motherhood can be incredibly exhausting, which means there is no time for mom to hang out with her friends and relax a little. When women experience postpartum depression, they don't particularly want to go out with their friends. You can change this dad, by setting up a surprise date for your partner and her friends. Offer to keep the baby, and ask her friends to stop by and persuade her to go out with them for a little while. If this idea doesn't work, you can try getting her to do something she enjoys, such as booking a spa day for her or taking her out for a movie on date night. It's important that your partner spends some time away from home so she can clear her mind and enjoy herself.

## *Taking Care of Your Newborn*

This topic was discussed in detail in the last chapter of the previous book as well, so we will briefly touch on the important points in this chapter. Fathers are notably oblivious when it comes to taking care of a newborn baby. Most people agree that this is because their paternal instincts haven't kicked in just yet, so they have no idea what their baby needs whenever they are crying and being fussy. A mother, on the other hand, knows exactly what to do and when to do it because of her maternal instincts. This fear often becomes the main reason why dads shirk away from their fatherly duties towards their babies. However, you are not going to be one of those scared fathers who refuse to learn and get over their fears, because you are ready to absorb as much knowledge as humanly possible! Here are some important tips you need to know about taking care of a newborn.

## *Tips for Helping With Feeding*

Yes, breastfeeding is a journey that moms undertake with their newborn baby, but who's to say that dads can't be a part of that journey too? There are many ways you can assist your wife during breastfeeding, especially during the first few weeks after the baby is born. Your willingness to actively participate and be a part of her journey, will bring you closer as a couple, and make breastfeeding a joyous experience.

- Learn as much as you can about breastfeeding. Do your research and use that information to make breastfeeding easier for your partner. You can also consult a lactation specialist or a nurse who is well versed in breastfeeding.

- While your partner is breastfeeding, offer to make her some tea or pour her a glass of water. It's vital that she stays hydrated to avoid falling ill, and so that her body can produce more milk for the baby.

- After the baby has been fed, offer to take the baby so you can burp them.

- If the baby has to spit up milk whilst feeding, help mom wipe the baby and change their clothes.

- If your baby is bottle-fed, you can help your partner take turns feeding the baby throughout the day.

- You can also help clean the bottles and sterilize them after every feed.

- Preparing baby's milk is another great way you can help. Measure the milk and store it away in containers. Pre-boil the water and keep warm in a flask. And make sure the dummies are sterilized before feeding.

## *Tips for Soothing*

A crying baby can be very difficult to handle. As a new dad, you might not know exactly what to do to calm your baby down. The key to soothing your baby lies in understanding the reason they're upset in the first place. It could be a number of different things, but here's a list of the most common reasons and how you can help calm your baby down.

## **Colic**

Colic is one of the most common reasons why babies cry inconsolably, especially during the first few weeks after birth. A baby who has colic will cry non-stop throughout the day, most frequently at night. The main cause of colic is when a baby's digestive system isn't fully developed yet.

This causes gas to become trapped in the intestines, and this can be extremely uncomfortable for babies. Colic can also be caused by food allergies and intolerances, and overfeeding as well. Here's what you can do to help your baby:

- Place the baby tummy first onto your lap, and gently rub their back. Sway your lap from side to side, as this can give the baby instant relief.

- Give your baby a teaspoon of Gripe water. Check with your pediatrician if it is okay first. Gripe water is safe and effective for treating colic in babies.

- Try swaddling your baby in their blanket. This can help place some pressure on the tummy, which can aid in releasing the gas.

- Consider giving your baby a warm, relaxing bath.

- Take your baby for a walk outside. Being out in nature can help distract the baby, and keep them calm.

- Give your baby their pacifier, and sing them a song to help calm them down.

## *Muscle or Neck Sprain*

Another common reason why babies cry so much is that they might have experienced a neck sprain. Remember, a baby's spine hasn't fully developed yet, which means that their neck muscles are still very weak. Parents can sometimes hurt their babies by mistake when lifting them off the bed, or whilst holding them during a bath. If you suspect that your baby has a neck sprain, then visit a doctor immediately. In this case, soothing your baby after visiting the doctor can be helpful.

- Hold your baby in an upright position against your shoulder, with one hand placed around the head and the neck for support, and another hand cradled under the baby's bottom.

- Sit on a rocking chair and sway your baby from back to front gently.

- Consider playing some relaxing music for your baby.

- Give your baby a massage. A nurse or doctor will show you what to do in this regard.

## Restless Baby

Sometimes, a baby will fuss and cry just because they haven't been able to have a good sleep. There are several reasons why this happens. Maybe your baby is still hungry, or maybe there is too much noise around you. Or maybe they can sense that mom or dad is upset and feeling a bit restless themselves. Surprisingly, babies pick up on the vibes that parents give off. Whatever the reasons might be, there are ways you can help soothe your baby when your partner is at their wit's end.

- Shift your baby to a quiet room where there is minimal noise.

- Give your baby a bottle feed, or allow mom to breastfeed for a while. Curbing hunger pangs can be helpful.

- Try to break your baby's wind by burping them. Sometimes this could be a reason why your baby is restless.

- You can place your baby down in their cot and put on their mobile toy with music.

- Change your baby's diaper. This is the reason why they are restless most of the time.

## *Going Out and About With Baby*

Traveling with a newborn is a real challenge, and it definitely takes two to get things moving! Dad, there are many ways you can help make traveling easier for both you and your partner. Here's how you can do this:

- Get the car seat prepped at least 10 minutes before leaving. Make sure that it is safely secured in the back seat. Double-check all the belts and clips, and put an extra blanket down so it will feel more comfortable for a newborn baby.

- Help your partner pack the baby's bag. Create a checklist and check off each item as you pack it. Don't forget to include the bottles, pacifiers, formula, and diapers.

- Get the stroller or pram ready, and put it into the boot of your car. Most parents forget about the strollers in a rush.

- When driving with a baby, make sure that the back doors are locked, and the windows are rolled up.

- Never leave your baby unattended in a car seat.

## *Segue*

This has been one long chapter dad! But it has taught you all you need to know about taking care of your new baby. Before you head on to the next chapter, take some time to briefly go over the main points in this chapter to help refresh your memory. Remember, fear is what holds you back from being an amazing dad to your newborn, so put all this new knowledge to good use, and eliminate the fear from your mind! In the next chapter, we focus more on the added roles and responsibilities of new dads, as well as the changes your baby will undergo over the next two months.

Chapter 2:

# Cute Little Fists and Cute Little Socks

## Everything You Need to Know About the Development of Your Baby Over the Next Two Months

Welcome to the next two months of your baby's development! There's so much more to learn, but don't worry dad, the journey gets more exciting! As your baby grows rapidly, there will be a couple of new responsibilities that will show up along the way. This chapter aims to equip you with as much knowledge as possible, so you can step into your new role as a confident father who is excited about being a part of your baby's journey. The first chapter would have helped you get over the majority of your fears surrounding the care of your baby.

## *Milestones and Changes in Your Baby During Month One*

The first month of your baby's life is the most crucial time in their development. Every baby is different, so each of them will develop at a different rate. Don't compare your little one's development to anyone else's. If you are concerned about your baby in any way, visit the doctor first before you make any assumptions of your own. You will learn more about the development of a baby within their first month in this section, so pay close attention. Your baby will grow up so fast, and you probably won't even remember all the changes they went through in the first month. So try not to be stressed all the time. Let yourself enjoy the experience. Your baby will jump from one month to one year before you even realize it, so slow down and pay attention to the little things. Here's what you should know about your baby's development in the first month.

### **Growth: How Fast is My Baby Growing?**

Although your baby might not look like it, they are actually growing a little every day. On average, babies should gain around 0.7-0.9kg in their first month. They will grow by 2.3cm to 4 cm, and the circumference of their head will increase by 1.25cm each month. Babies tend to lose weight after they are born, but they manage to get back to their birth weight within a few weeks, and from there on out its continuous growth. Now, it's important that you remember not all babies are the same. Each child's growth is determined by a number of different factors, so it would be good to focus only on your own child's development. Your baby's growth will be monitored by nurses who will record their weight and height at every check-up. If the healthcare professionals notice that your baby isn't growing properly, they will ask more questions to find out if there is anything in particular that might be causing a problem. However, they usually give it a few weeks before they see any need to be concerned.

One of the key ways you can track your baby's growth is by watching how they fit into their clothing. Within the first month, your newborn will be ready to fit into clothing sizes 0-3 months. Their tiny little feet will become a bit plumper, and their little fingers will grow longer. Sometimes, parents miss out on these one-month growth signs because they are still recovering from pregnancy and childbirth. They simply wake up one morning and notice that their baby looks a bit different, and they have no idea how it happened. It can be a bit difficult to notice these growth changes physically in your baby in their first month, but rest assured, there is a lot of growth happening behind the scenes.

## *Motor Skills: What Can My Baby Do at One Month?*

There isn't much your baby can do at one-month-old. Their reflexes are still developing, so their motor skills won't be as sharp as you might expect. The cute movements they can do are narrowed down to sucking, swallowing, looking for milk by moving their mouths, and kicking out their arms and legs. Babies aren't really thinking about their movements right now as they are still developing. Some babies are more chill, and they prefer to lay around staring at mom and dad without making much of an effort. While others are very active since day one—moving their tiny little feet and hands around with their fists clenched tightly. By the time your baby reaches one month, they will be able to follow an object with their eyes. If you had to hold a toy in front of them and move it slowly from side to side, your baby would be able to follow that object with their eyes. Don't worry if your baby can't do it just yet. They might need a few more weeks to develop their motor skills, and this is completely normal.

I'm sure you must have heard about babies smiling as soon as they escaped from their mom's uterus. Well, as crazy as it sounds, it's very much possible! Babies develop their facial muscles when they're in the womb, and most of them are caught smiling on 3D ultrasound scans. Watching your baby smile at you whenever they hear your voice is a magical experience that many parents look forward to. Your baby will be able to smile by the time they reach one month old, so don't worry dad, those magical moments will be happening soon! Apart from their cute little side smiles, your baby can also do another exciting trick! When you place your baby's feet down on a flat surface, for instance when you are carrying them under their torso and their feet are on your lap, they will move one foot in front of the other. You'd be surprised at the strength those tiny legs have, especially with all the practice they had in the womb kicking mom every hour! In addition to those strong feet, your baby will learn how to put their fingers in their mouth to soothe themselves. This would be a good time to introduce a pacifier if you haven't already done so.

### *Sleep: When Will My Baby Find a Sleep Routine?*

Sleep! Oh, how much you miss it, dad. These first few weeks have been the worst when it comes to getting any form of sleep. You probably spent hours awake at night on baby duty, changing diapers, making bottles, and shushing your little one back to sleep. This sleep deprivation must have turned you into a zombie, and the only thing that can help you now is a good night's rest. Newborns usually sleep around 15-20 hours a day because it's all they ever did whilst in the womb. However, there are some babies who are adjusting to life outside the womb, and sleep isn't on the itinerary for them over the next few weeks. As your baby approaches one month, their sleeping patterns will change. They will begin to understand the difference between day and night, and so their sleep schedule will be focused on that.

Your baby picks up on sounds and light, so they will recognize that it's daytime when there is more light in the room, and when there is more activity going on in terms of noise. They will recognize that it's nighttime when it becomes quieter and darker in the room. Parents sometimes interfere with their babies' sleep routines by keeping the lights on in the room at night, and not maintaining a quiet atmosphere. When there is activity gouging around your baby, they will not sleep well. However, if you are doing whatever it takes to make sure that your baby is falling into a good sleep routine, then rest assured, by the end of month one they will be getting used to the idea of sleep. Your baby will still awake at night for a feed, or for a quick diaper change, so be on alert when you hear those cries.

## *What You Can Do to Help Your Baby Develop*

Dads, the answer to this question lies with you. First, ask yourself how much time you can spend with your baby. If you want to help your baby develop well, you must be willing to make the time for it. The truth is, the more time you spend with your baby, the more impact you will have on their development. When you look into your baby's eyes, you bond with them and make them feel secure. Smiling at your baby makes them feel confident that they are safe. Your presence makes a lot of difference in your baby's development, and most parents don't realize this. There are many things you can do to help your baby learn new skills. The first thing you can do is sing to your baby. Music helps stimulate your baby's senses. Your voice helps calm your baby when they are upset, and it creates a familiarity so that every time your child hears your voice they know that it's you. Reading is another great activity you can do with your one-month-old baby. Of course, they wouldn't be able to understand what you are saying, but they can see your facial expressions and hear your voice. You can also play with toys and talk to your baby at the same time. Puppet shows are a good example of developmental activities. Your baby can learn how to follow objects with their eyes, and they can see different colors on these toys.

At just one month old, your baby's neck hasn't fully developed yet. You can perform an exercise with your baby to help them build strength in their neck. Place your baby down on their tummy on the bed or on the floor. Leave them in that position for a little while (1-5 mins). This exercise is known as tummy time, and it helps your baby learn how to slowly pick their neck up. A few minutes a day is all it takes, but please don't leave your baby alone during tummy time. If your baby falls asleep during tummy time, put them to sleep on their back so they don't suffocate with their face pressed down on the bed or on the floor.

## Developmental Problems Signs to Look Out For at 1 Month Old

As we mentioned previously, each baby is different, so they will develop in their own time and reach their milestones when they are ready. Parents work themselves up by comparing their children to others, not realizing that there are a number of factors that come into play which determine how fast your baby develops. However, you can still be patient with your baby and keep an eye out for any developmental problems simultaneously. Here are the signs you should look out for in your one-month-old baby which could point to a developmental issue.

- You notice that your baby isn't feeding well. It's been a few weeks since birth and their feeding hasn't improved. Babies usually drink milk after every two hours or so. If your baby is having trouble swallowing or keeping the milk down, then you should visit the doctor.

- Your baby sleeps more than 16 hours a day regularly. They might not even wake up for their feed.

- They aren't moving their legs or their arms, and they've already reached one month of age.

- When your baby sees you or hears your voice, they don't respond. Their eyes don't follow an object when you move it in front of them.

- Your baby isn't making any gurgling sounds with their mouth.

- Your baby doesn't become startled when there is a sudden loud sound.

- You notice that your baby is crying continuously for days on end, and they aren't sleeping well.

### *Sample Schedule for a One-Month-Old Baby*

Developing a routine for your baby as a new parent can be difficult. Because you have no prior experience, you don't particularly understand why setting a routine is important for both you and your baby. During the first few weeks after birth, your baby will be busy adjusting to the environment they are living in. This will be a good time to introduce a schedule. Below, you will find a sample schedule for a one-month-old baby. You can take inspiration from it and create your own schedule for your baby.

**7:45 a.m.** (Rise and Shine)-This is the time your baby should wake up in the morning.

**8:00 a.m.** (Feeding)-Your baby will have their first feed for the day.

**8:30–9:00 a.m.** (Awake time)-This is when your baby will be awake in their crib or in their baby chair. You can talk to your baby, or play music for them while you are getting ready for the day. Most parents prefer to bathe their babies during this time.

**9:00–11:00 a.m.** (Nap 1): Your baby will have their first nap for the day during this time. It's usually known as the morning nap.

**11:00 a.m.** (Feeding): When your baby wakes up, they will be hungry so offer a feed during this time.

**11:30–12:00 p.m.** (Awake time): If you haven't bathed your baby in the morning, you can set aside this time to do so. Alternatively, you can take your baby for a walk in their stroller, or do something fun with them.

**12:00–2:00 p.m.** (Nap 2): Also known as the mid-day nap. Most babies prefer to sleep during this time, so try to keep this nap time in your own routine. Ensure that there is minimal noise around your baby so that their sleep doesn't get disturbed.

**2:00 p.m.** (Feeding): Your baby will require another feed when they wake up from their afternoon nap.

**2:30–3:00 p.m.** (Awake time): This is the time of day when your baby will be left to their own devices. Allow your child to spend some time in their crib alone, so they can discover the world around them. Don't carry your baby too much because they develop a habit which Indian mother's like to refer to as "hand habit". This is when your baby refuses to be put down, and this can make life very hard for new parents.

**3:00–5:00 p.m.** (Nap 3): This is known as the afternoon nap. Most babies are tempted to sleep through their two hours of nap time, but please don't let this happen, dad! The more your baby sleeps in the afternoon, the longer it will take for them to go to sleep at night.

**5:00 p.m.** (Feeding): Another feed will be given as soon as the baby wakes up.

**5:30–6:30 p.m.** (Awake time): Keep activity minimal during the evening so your baby can understand that it's time to wind down for the day. Play some music, and talk to your baby about how your day went.

**6:30–7:00 p.m.** (Nap time): This nap must only be 30 minutes long. If your baby sleeps too long, they will go to bed a lot later than they are supposed to.

**7:00–7:30/8 p.m.** (Awake time): This is a good time to do some winding-down activities with your baby. A nice warm bath would be nice, followed by a relaxing massage. Read your baby a story and get them ready for bed.

**8:00 p.m.** (Bedtime): Put your baby down for the night. Keep the nursery quiet and minimally lit. Hereafter, your baby will awaken every two to three hours for a feed.

**Nighttime feeds**: 10:00 p.m./2:00 a.m./4:00 a.m./6–7 a.m.

## *Milestones and Changes of a Baby During Month Two*

Wow dad! Your baby is now two months old! As the weeks pass by, your little one is slowly moving away from the newborn stage. You might have noticed that your baby has become a bit more active. There are new milestones to reach during month two, and your baby is getting ready to achieve all of them. You and your partner might still experience some exhaustion, only because your bodies are still adjusting to the new routine you have developed. Be patient with your baby, and with yourself. It takes time to adjust to this new life you have going on. Here's how your baby should be developing during month two.

### *Growth: How Fast is My Baby Growing?*

Your baby is growing very fast dad! During month two, your baby will grow up to 1 ½ inches more, and their weight will increase by at least 1 kg. Their facial features will become more defined and plumped out by now, and they will look less like a newborn and more like a baby. Their little arms and legs will begin to develop rolls as your baby puts on more weight. However, don't be alarmed if your baby isn't looking a little fatty just yet. Some babies take a while before they start packing on the pounds, especially if they are being breastfed. On average, your baby should be gaining around 1kg every month. If your baby is having trouble latching on to the breasts, then it could have an effect on the amount of milk they receive per feed. This could be a reason why your baby isn't putting on weight. If this is the case with your baby, consider seeking the help of a lactation specialist.

## Motor Skills: What Can My Baby Do at Two Months?

There is a lot your baby can do at two months old! Your little nugget is getting stronger each day, which means that their muscles and reflexes are improving. As a result, their movements are less jerky and more intentional. Some babies even reach out their hands to grab onto mom or dad's face. Their tiny body is working overtime, with all the kicking and punching that's going on. Because of this increase in activity, your baby will feel tired more regularly, and their appetite will increase as well. If your baby is breastfed, they will become hungrier much faster than if they were formula fed. This is because breast milk digests quicker than formula, leaving little babies wanting more and more. When you place your baby down on their belly for tummy time, you will notice that they can lift their heads up more easily, and they can even move their head from side to side following sounds and watching mom or dad.

Another exciting development to make a note of is that your little nugget is making lots of gurgling sounds with their mouth, and it almost seems like they are talking! Get ready to hear a whole lot of cooing and gurgling sounds dad, your baby is just getting started! At two months old, your baby will be using their cries to try and communicate their needs with you and your partner, so pay attention to them when they cry so you can develop an understanding of what your baby needs and when. Their digestive system would have settled into a routine by now, as your baby feeds on time throughout the day. You will be able to tell when your baby is hungry and when they need to poop! This is quite helpful when you are on daddy duty, as most fathers get caught off guard by their baby's diaper bombs. All in all, month two is simply an upgrade from month one. Whatever skills your baby developed during month one, will be heightened a little more during month two.

## *Sleep: How Will My Baby Sleep at Two Months?*

You're probably missing your sleep a lot by now dad, and I'm afraid that there's no good news in the sleep department just yet. As much as you want your little one to fall into a sleep routine, it's going to take some time before that happens. Most babies adjust to their schedules and routines by month three, which is why they manage to sleep better at night when they reach this age. The duration of the daytime naps will gradually decrease, and the duration of their nighttime sleep will increase as they become familiar with a routine. Dads, this is why it is so important that you and your partner develop a routine for your baby to follow during the day so that they will be able to sleep better at night. When you deter from this routine, it could cause a disturbance in your baby's sleeping patterns which is never good for you or your baby. The sample routine schedule provided in the first section can be implemented in the second month as well. There might only be a slight change in the length of time your baby is awake since they are more active now.

## *What You Can Do to Help Your Baby Develop*

Here are some of the things you can do to help your baby develop at two months old. As your baby grows, they will spend more time awake during the day. This means that you, dad, will have to find ways to keep your baby entertained! You can spend time doing activities that help them develop. Here are some activities you can do to help your baby.

- Take your baby out of the house for walks. It's important for them to adapt to the world around them. Let them look at the birds and the other animals like the dogs and cats which play at the park.

- Tummy time is still a great activity to do with your baby. You can increase the duration of tummy time to 10 minutes—depending on how well your baby has adjusted.

- Massage the baby regularly. This helps to strengthen their muscles and ease any aches they might have from being held all the time.

- Smile and talk to your baby. This helps build social skills and enhances the bond between parent and child.

## *Developmental Problems to Look Out for in Your Two-Month-Old*

Here's what developmental problems you should keep an eye out for in your two-month-old baby. Catching it earlier on in your baby's development is always better.

- It's already been eight weeks and your baby isn't smiling yet.

- Your baby doesn't calm down, not even for a minute when you pick them up to soothe them during a crying episode.

- You notice that one side of their body is much stronger than the other side.

- They don't become startled when sudden noises appear.

- Their fingers are still grasped into tight fists.

- They haven't been drinking milk properly.

If you notice any of these signs in your baby, please visit the doctor as soon as you can. Don't listen to the advice of family and friends who try to downplay your baby's symptoms just because they had a few kids and think they know what they're talking about. A medical opinion is always better, so listen to your gut dad.

## *Your Roles and Responsibilities as a Working Dad*

Being the head of the household comes with many responsibilities. Fathers tend to miss out on spending quality time with their babies because of work, however, they do have certain responsibilities which they have to fulfill. Raising your baby takes the hard work of two parents. Even if you are the sole breadwinner in the home, you still have a role to play in your baby's life. In this modern age, a lot has changed for dads. They are more involved in their children's lives, and they actively participate in their development. Your role as a dad is no longer limited to bringing home the bacon. Here's what you can do to embrace your new role and responsibilities of fatherhood.

### *Accept Your New Role*

Life has changed since the moment you found out that you are going to be a dad. All the plans you had made for the near future suddenly came to a halt because you now have to accommodate a new chapter in your life—raising your child. Most fathers begin to experience anxiety attacks early on in the pregnancy because they are afraid of giving up their own plans for their own lives. Being a father means you have to grow up and put aside your childish ways so you can be the man that your partner and your baby need. This can only happen once you accept your new role as a dad. Your mind and your heart need to be aligned so that you can embrace your "fatherly" duties with excitement and ease. If you aren't ready mentally and emotionally, you will never be able to fulfill your responsibilities as a father.

You have to realize that fatherhood comes with a lot of emotions. The good emotions such as excitement, joy, happiness, and love, come with the bad emotions such as anxiety, fear, and stress. If you understand what your job entails as a father, you will be able to prepare yourself mentally, emotionally, and physically. Knowing that you are well-prepared, you'll have that extra kick of confidence in yourself as a new dad. Confidence helps ease your anxiety, allowing you to spend more time with your little one, as opposed to being afraid and staying away from your baby because of a lack of confidence in yourself.

## *Write About Your Feelings*

It's difficult for men to talk about their feelings, especially when they are going through a major life change. Raising a baby is no joke, and fathers also have to deal with their insecurities just like moms do. It always helps to talk to someone about your feelings, but if you don't feel like being vulnerable around other people, there is an alternative way to get things off your chest. Consider keeping a journal where you can write about your feelings, your fears, and your insecurities. Journals are a great tool to help you sort through your emotions in private. Reflecting back on your journal entries after a few days helps you see things from a different perspective. The best thing about having a journal is you don't have to worry about being judged by anyone! Your journal can hold your deepest secrets without staring at you in squinty disgust. Whenever you feel anxious or stressed out about your role as a father, take a few minutes to sit down and write about your feelings. Elaborate on what's making you feel anxious, and make a note of the events which led up to your anxiety attack. This can help you keep an eye out for those same events in the future which give rise to your anxiety.

As you continue confiding in your journal about your feelings, you will notice how much more confident you will become in yourself as a dad. If you feel like you aren't getting anywhere by writing in your journal, then you should consider visiting a therapist who can help you, using different methods. There is no shame in seeking help for your own mental and emotional well-being, because a responsible father will do whatever it takes to make sure that he is healthy enough to take care of his baby. There are also journal apps that you can download on your smartphone, so you don't have to worry about carrying a book and pen around all the time.

**Say Goodbye to Your Own Expectations About our Own Identity**

Prior to becoming a father, you must have had your own expectations of what your future would look like. Maybe you fantasized about fatherhood being a blissful journey of cuddles and kisses with your newborn baby. But now, you are faced with sleepless nights and constant crying that just won't stop. Because dads don't know what fatherhood is really about, they unknowingly create a picture in their minds of what they think fatherhood should be like. This causes more harm than good. It's time to say goodbye to your old expectations about your identity as a father and embrace the new role of fatherhood that you have in front of you right now. It's the only way you will ever be able to be the father your little baby needs. Apart from having unrealistic expectations of fatherhood, there is another aspect that many dads struggle with when they become a parent—their past identity.

Before your baby could arrive, you were a different person. You probably weren't as mature as you are now, and life was less complicated then. Now you have all this responsibility, and you aren't sure whether you fit the profile of a father. All those thoughts and insecurities hold you back from stepping into your new role with confidence. Let go of the past version of yourself! There is a new and improved role waiting for you. And yes! You do have everything it takes to be an amazing dad. Believe in yourself, and don't be afraid to make changes to accommodate your new role. Your baby needs you, so say goodbye to the old you, and get ready to embrace this new chapter of your life!

*Create New Habits*

Once you become a parent, there's so much you have to change about yourself. This includes your good habits and your bad habits! Mothers aren't the only ones who have to give up so much of themselves so that they can have more time to spend with their baby—fathers have to give up parts of themselves as well. This often includes leaving behind your old habits and routines so you can create new ones which include your baby. Say for instance, before your baby arrived, you always played video games before bedtime, and you loved waking up late during the weekends. But now that your baby is here, you have to change these habits so you can make time for your baby.

No more waking up late over the weekend because you now have new responsibilities to see to. Instead, you can discuss with your partner and agree to set aside a day when she gets to sleep in while you take care of the baby and vice versa. This is a new habit you can create that will benefit both you and your family. You don't have to get rid of your old habits entirely. You can simply tweak them to suit the needs of your new family.

## *Segue*

Now that you are well-versed in the development of your baby during the first two months, it's time to focus on the next couple of months. In the next chapter, you will learn more about your growing baby, and discover ways to maintain your work life and your family life amidst the sleep loss cycle.

Chapter 3:

# Smiling Babies, Sleepless Dads!

## Finding Balance in Your Home and Work Life While Your Baby Continues Developing

> *There are no words to describe the euphoria you feel when your baby recognizes you for the first time and smiles.* –Jared Padalecki

Welcome to months three and four of your baby's life! There are many exciting developments taking place during the third month, and you don't want to miss any of them! This chapter aims to help you learn all about the changes taking place with your baby in the upcoming months, so you can prepare yourself for what to expect. You will also learn key ways to balance your hectic lifestyle with work on one side, and a new baby on the other side. These strategies will help you sail through your responsibilities without becoming lost under the waves of chaos.

## *Milestones and Changes in Your Baby at Three Months*

Three months old is considered a milestone age for babies because of their spike in development. It's shocking how fast your baby went from being a newborn to a three-month-old who can smile, and can recognize mom and dad's faces! There's a lot you need to know about how your baby develops during the third month, and you also have a role to play in their incredible journey of growth. This section will provide you with all the vital information you need to better understand how your baby develops during month three.

### Growth: How Fast is My Baby Growing?

Your baby will be growing at a rapid rate, and they will be packing on the pounds by now. On average, a three-month-old baby should weigh around 5.2 kg, and you probably would have noticed those cute little rolls appear on their thighs, and their chubby cheeks begin bursting with cuteness. These are all tell-tale signs that your baby is putting on weight. However, if you notice that your baby isn't putting on enough weight, or if you are concerned that they might be putting on too much weight, then you should consider taking your baby to a doctor to make sure that they are growing well. In certain instances, babies who gain a lot of weight during the first six months, are at risk for becoming obese later on in their adult lives, so pay attention to their weight gain and don't force your baby to drink more milk just because you feel they haven't had enough.

## *Motor Skills: What Can My Baby Do at Three Months?*

Once your baby reaches three months of age, they will begin to experience emotions for the first time. They will feel different emotions such as sadness, happiness, fear, and a little bit of anger too—especially when you do something they don't like! Despite having all of these emotions, your baby will only be able to communicate their feelings in two ways—crying and laughing. Apart from experiencing emotions, your baby will be able to recognize familiar faces! That's right, dad! Your baby can now tell the difference between mommy and daddy, and they will give you a nice big smile to let you know that they like you very much. When you place a toy in your baby's hand, they will be able to swish the toy from side to side. They will also try to grasp any objects that are dangling in front of them. For instance, when you hold a toy in front of your baby, they will reach out to try and grab it. When you place your baby on a flat surface, they will lift their legs in excitement and kick out their little feet. Some parents have even experienced their babies turning over onto one side at just three months old! This is why it's crucial that you never leave your baby alone.

Another incredible development that your baby will experience is hand and eye coordination. They will be able to bring their hands up towards their mouth, and you will notice their eyes watching their hands while they are doing this. Your baby will also turn their heads whenever they hear a familiar voice or a sound coming from the radio or TV. Don't be alarmed if you hear little babbling sounds, that's your baby learning how to become more vocal! These cute little sounds made by your baby will melt your heart and keep you glued to them all day. Along with their "talkative" nature, your baby will also throw in a couple of facial expressions whilst they're at it—opening their eyes wider, or scrunching up their tiny little noses. It becomes much more enjoyable to play with your baby, now that they can understand you a little better.

## Sleep: How Will My Baby Sleep at Three Months?

Most babies who had trouble sleeping during the first two months after birth will find their sleep routine by the time they reach three months of age. This is because they spend most of their time awake and alert during the day. Because they want to learn more about their surroundings, they keep themselves awake to explore. This makes your baby feel very tired, which means they will sleep longer at night. However, it's important to note that it might take a while before their sleeping patterns become normal. There will be nights when your baby just doesn't want to sleep at all! They will go to bed at 8:30 p.m., and you will dance with joy thinking that your little one is going to sleep through the night. But then you find them awake in their crib at 10:00 p.m., talking to themselves and staring at their toys. It's best if you just take each day as it comes because your baby's sleep schedule is still unpredictable at this age. There will be good nights, when you manage to get some sleep, and there will be bad nights when you stay up all night with your baby. This is how fatherhood is for the first couple of months, but I can promise you that it will get better with time. As long as you have patience, you will be able to beat your frustration and handle your exhaustion better.

## What Can I Do to Help My Baby Develop?

From three months onwards, your baby's language skills are being developed. You can help develop these skills by reading to your baby. Continue to talk to your baby, and enhance your facial expressions to support what you are saying. Make different sounds with your mouth when you are talking about animals or vehicles. This grabs your baby's attention, and keeps them focused on you. Communication is important, so try your best to make it exciting for your baby. Another great activity you can still do with your baby is tummy time! Tummy time is still a very important activity, especially now that your baby has turned three months old. When your baby is on their tummy, it sets the perfect foundation for them to learn how to push themselves to the limit. They move their hands and legs to support their body weight while they try to push themselves up. Their neck muscles also develop during tummy time, as your baby tries to pick their head up and look around the room. You can also do some light exercises with your baby when they wake up in the morning. Place your baby down on the bed, or on the floor on a soft blanket, with their backs facing down. Gently move each leg up and down a few times, almost as if they are riding a bicycle. Next, take each arm and gently stretch them up over your baby's head, and then bring them back down again. This is great for helping the muscles stretch and warm up for the development of your growing baby.

## *Developmental Problems to Look Out for in Your Three-Month Old*

- Your baby has trouble moving either one or both of their eyes in different directions.

- When you dangle objects in front of your baby, they don't reach out to grasp them.

- During tummy time, your baby has difficulty picking their head up, even slightly.

- Your baby doesn't smile when they hear your voice, or when they see you.

- You notice that your baby is crossing their eyes a lot.

- When you place your baby's feet down on a flat surface, they don't press against it.

- Your baby's appetite has decreased, and they are refusing milk for days.

## *Milestones and Changes in Your Baby at Four Months*

Welcome to month four of your baby's life! It's been an exhausting journey thus far, but I'm sure you must have enjoyed spending every minute with your new baby, dad! Just two months more before your baby turns 6-months old (which is basically half a year old). There's a lot of growing going on, and you probably haven't noticed it because you still think of your baby as that little newborn you brought home from the hospital all those months ago. However, there's a lot taking place behind the scenes! Let's take a deeper look into how your baby is developing at four months.

### *Growth: How Fast is My Baby Growing?*

Your baby is growing at a steady pace from month to month, which you might have noticed from their outgrown leggings. Their average weight should be around 6.7 kg—one more kg since last month! Your little baby has gotten a bit plumper than last month, and you can feel it when you carry them. It's time to put away the baby booties because your sweet pie's feet have grown significantly longer! You can keep track of your baby's growth by placing one of their feet against the palm of your hand. It's easier to see how fast their feet have been growing, using this method. Along with your baby's physical developments, there is another very important part that is developing very quickly as well—your baby's brain. How do you think your baby has learned to recognize you, or to smile whenever you do something funny? It's all thanks to their intelligent little brain, which is growing each day. Your baby's facial features will appear more defined, and they will start looking more like mommy or daddy by now.

### *Motor Skills: What Can My Baby Do?*

In month four, your baby will be able to do a lot more than they could in month three. For starters, let's talk about their ability to hold their neck up themselves now, without much help from mom or dad. However, it's imperative that you keep your hands behind your baby's neck, as a precaution, in case they suddenly jump backward. Keep an eye on your baby when you leave them to play on the bed because your tiny tot has finally learned how to roll over! Within a few weeks' time, your baby has gone from turning on their sides and grabbing their toes to completely rolling themselves over. In addition to this, your baby can also shake the toys that are in their hand, and even put them in their mouth, so be cautious about the toys your little one is playing with.

### *Sleep: How Will My Baby Sleep at Four Months?*

You should be sleeping a lot better at night, dad, since your baby is resting well from all that activity they are involved in during the day. Sleep is an important aspect of your baby's development, so it's crucial that you get them into a routine as soon as possible. If your baby doesn't sleep well at night, they will be a lot more crabby and irritable during the day. This is a sign that you need to pay more attention to developing a sleep schedule for your little one. If your baby is struggling to stay asleep at night, consider changing the ambiance of the room. Dim the lights, reduce all noise, give your baby a soothing massage, or sing a relaxing lullaby to them. These tips should help relax your baby enough to keep them asleep for longer. Here is a sample sleep schedule for a baby aged 3-4 months. Keep in mind that each child is different, and they all have their own needs and preferences. Your baby's sleep schedule could vary a bit, and that's fine. In time, your baby will fall into a routine, so be a little patient.

7:00 a.m.—Awake time

8:30 a.m.—Nap

9:30 a.m.—Awake

11:00 a.m.—Nap

12:00 p.m.—Awake

1:30 p.m.—Nap

3:00 p.m.—Awake

4:30 p.m.—Nap

5:30 p.m.—Awake

6:30 p.m.—Bedtime routine

7:00 p.m.—Bedtime

## What Can I Do to Help My Baby Develop?

You can cuddle with your baby, and spend time talking to them. Play with your baby, and teach them how to make different facial expressions. Encourage vocal development by making sounds such as "ooh," "eee," "ahhh," and saying words such as "wow" and "yay." Put your baby down to play, on the floor, with a soft blanket to keep them comfortable. Place all their toys around them, and leave them to play on their own. Don't carry your baby all the time, because this will create attachment issues which also affect development. Teach your baby independence from a young age by allowing them to explore on their own.

## Developmental Problems to Look Out For in Your Four-Month-Old

- Your baby does not turn over on their side or roll over on their tummy without your help.
- You notice that your baby doesn't smile at people, or at any familiar faces.
- When you leave your baby down to play, they cry uncontrollably.
- Your baby cannot hold up their head by themselves.
- Your baby is sleeping more than 12 hours a day on a regular basis.
- They haven't been making any sounds with their mouths.
- They don't bring their hands up to their mouth.

## *Balancing Work and Baby as a New Dad*

Being a father in this modern world is quite different from being a dad in the 70s or 80s! There is a lot more responsibility placed on dads nowadays, and moms have expectations that their partner will be an active part of their baby's life. Research shows that children with fathers who are actively involved in their lives, have a lower risk of becoming involved with drugs, alcohol, and violence (Bedortha, 2020). This means that they are less likely to end up in prison. The role of a father is one of great importance in a child's life. This doesn't mean that a mother cannot provide for children, or raise them well—there are plenty of single mothers out there raising great children on their own. But the presence of a loving father, who takes an initiative in raising his children, has an incredible impact on the type of people his children become later on in life. Gone are the days when dads just went to work, and moms stayed home taking care of the children. Nowadays, men and women have switched roles! There are working-class moms who go to work, and stay-at-home dads who help with the cooking and cleaning and taking care of the children. Even if both parents are working, fathers are still expected to come home after work and help mom with the baby. This includes bathing, feeding, changing diapers, reading to them, and putting them to bed. This can be a lot to balance for a new dad, especially when he has to work all day.

The pressures of working a full-time job can be so overwhelming at times that most dads carry that stress with them, and then take it out on their families when they get home. They become so distracted that they cannot spend quality time with their babies, nor do they want to help mom out around the house. Eventually, these dads lose out on the most precious moments with their babies because of the inability to balance work life and home life. You have the chance to make the best of these moments with your new baby, without having to worry about what's going on at work. Below, there are a couple of amazing tips you can apply to your daily life to ensure that you are creating a balance between work and home effectively.

### *Don't Bring Work Home With You*

Whatever happens at work, must stay at work. Don't make the mistake of bringing your work home with you, because this is jeopardizing time with your family. When you leave for work each day, you aren't taking anything from home with you—except for your lunch. You are focused on your job throughout the day, and you are away from your family during that time. Think about it this way; you aren't changing diapers in the office, or cooking supper for your family during lunch, so why would you take work home when you're supposed to be spending it with your family? Keep your work life separate from your home life—that's how you create a balance. When the two worlds mix, discord, and chaos erupts. As soon as you step into your home, leave everything work related outside the door. Give your wife and your baby your full attention when you are at home.

### *Turn off Your Phone and De-Stress*

Another important point to remember when you are trying to create a balance between work and home life, is to always switch off your phone, or leave it aside when you are spending time with your baby. Phones have a way of grabbing your attention, and if you spend most of your time glued to your screen, you miss out on that quality time with your baby. Also, make it known to your work colleagues that you will not be accepting calls or replying to messages once you leave work.

Only in the case of an emergency, they are allowed to call you. As for all that stress you have been accumulating throughout the day at work, please make sure that you leave it outside the door when you come home. This stress will hold you back from being the dad you want to be, so try your best to de-stress before you come home. You could sit in your car for a few minutes, before you enter the house, and do some deep breathing exercises. Release the pent-up stress and frustration before you engage with your family. Think about your baby, and how they make you feel. Hold on to that warm feeling, and take that with you when you enter your home after a long day at work. It will allow you to be more open and loving towards your family.

*Enjoy Every Moment*

Immerse yourself in every activity you do with your baby. Don't be distracted by unnecessary things, instead, keep your focus on your baby. Dad, you must remember that your baby isn't going to remain this little for much longer. They are growing every day, and soon, your baby will be running around the house trying to avoid bedtime. The first 12 months are the only time you have to really enjoy your baby. Get lost in their amazing presence, cuddle as much as you can, and carry your baby in your arms because soon they will be too big to fit in your hands. Enjoy every moment you share with your baby, and keep your focus on being the best dad you can be. Don't have any regrets later on that you didn't spend enough time with your child because you were distracted by work all the time. Think of each moment you spend with your baby, as a gift that only lasts a while. You will learn to appreciate it more when you think of it that way.

## Ask for Help

It doesn't hurt to ask your family and close friends for help with your baby. If you have had a long day at work, and you really cannot manage to help your partner with the chores or with your baby, then consider asking a relative or a friend to help you take care of the baby for a little while. When people offer to help, accept it and don't feel guilty about taking help from family and friends. It's important that your partner also has time for themselves because self-care is very important. You also need a break from time to time, so you can energize yourself physically and mentally. Even fathers are at risk of burnout, and the best way you can avoid this is by making time for yourself. There has to be a balance within you first before you try to create balance in the world around you.

## Paternity Leave

Talk to your employer about their regulations on paternity leave. Find out whether your company offers paid paternity leave, and then talk with your partner about it. Most companies offer unpaid paternity leave, which makes it rather difficult for dads who want to spend time with their newborn babies. If you're the sole provider in the home, unpaid paternity leave could place undue stress on your finances. Choosing between going to work to provide for your family or spending time with your baby is an unfair decision many fathers have to make. Most dads choose to go to work instead of taking the unpaid paternity leave, whilst others have no choice but to stay home so that they can take care of their partner and their baby after delivery. Paid paternity leave, on the other hand, is a great benefit because you don't have to choose between providing for your family or spending time with your baby.

*Finances*

The arrival of a new baby means there is an added strain on your finances. This is why couples are encouraged to save up some money before they decide to have a baby, so there's less strain on their finances. It takes a lot of planning and commitment to ensure that you have enough money to see to your baby's needs once they get here. It would be wise to cut down on your unnecessary spending, as you can save that money for a rainy day. Also, buy baby stuff in bulk as it is a lot cheaper. If your family and friends wish to pass on baby clothing to you, accept it. You can save a lot of money by doing this. Baby clothes are quite expensive and they don't wear them for long because they grow so fast. Think of ways you can save money, so you don't have to put too much strain on your finances.

*Less Social Time*

Dads enjoy spending time with the guys, even if it's just one evening over the weekend. Chilling with your friends and bonding over a cold one is a must for every guy at least once a week or so. But when the baby gets here, life could get pretty hectic. You wouldn't be able to tell the difference between night and day with the lack of sleep you've been experiencing. Where would you find the time to hang out with your friends? Maybe during the first few weeks, it would be impossible to see your friends because you would be caught up in taking care of your partner and the baby. However, once your baby grows, it's important for you to go out and spend time with your friends. This is important to maintain a balance in your life. Also, make time to spend with your partner. Go for lunch, visit the movies and go out dancing to relieve some of that stress. It is important for balance.

## *Segue*

In this chapter, you have come to recognize and comprehend the developments taking place within your baby over months three and four. In the next chapter, we will explore further developments in months five and six of your baby's life.

# Chapter 4: Bonding With Your Babbling Baby

## Dads Need to Bond Too!

*The fact that the infant's babbling itself plays a role in future language development shows how important the interchange between parent and child is.* –Kuhl

In this chapter, we explore the development of your baby as they enter months five and six. This is a crucial time for your baby as they develop the most during these two months. You will also learn amazing tips on how to bond with your baby as a new dad!

## *Milestones and Changes in Your Baby at Five Months*

Welcome to month five of your baby's life! Just one more month before your baby turns half a year old. Wow, this has been an amazing journey thus far! As with the other chapters, we will be taking a look at how well your baby is developing during month five. There is much to learn about, so let's get started!

## *Growth: How Fast is My Baby Growing in Month Five?*

Your bouncing little baby should have doubled their birth weight by now, weighing in at a whopping 7.5kg! They would have outgrown most of their tiny clothing—which means that they're also getting taller. Your baby would have grown another inch in height by the time they have reached five months of age. It's incredible to see how fast your little one is developing. Their hair is probably a bit longer as well, and if you have a girl, you can put cute little headbands on her. Be cautious about putting little grips and dinkies in front of your baby as they could easily get a hold of it and put it into their mouth. All in all, your baby has grown quite a bit over the past month.

## *Motor Skills: What Can My Baby Do?*

At five months old, your baby can control their body a lot more now. They would be kicking their legs a lot more now and moving their arms around in excitement. You will notice how excited your baby is by the way they move their body. Along with all this moving of the hands and feet, your baby is also very eager to show off their personality! That's right dad, your baby has started developing their own personality, and it's getting sharper by the day. Your baby's eyesight and hearing have developed quite a bit as well by now, as they can see further than they could before. They can now tell the difference between several colors, and they focus better without crossing their eyes. As for your baby's speech, you will be hearing a lot of babbling going on dad, so prepare to get your babble on as well! Babbling is great for speech development, so encourage your baby to babble as much as they want.

## *Sleep: How Will My Baby Sleep at Five Months?*

During five months of age, your baby will still be sleeping most of the time. They will need plus or minus 10 hours of sleep each night, and another four hours of sleep during the day (naps) so they can grow and develop well. This is why you shouldn't wake a baby when they're sleeping. Sleep safety is very important, and it's safer to place your baby on their back, instead of on their tummy. Their crib should also be free from toys, blankets, and teddy bears. Infants are at risk for SIDS (sudden infant death syndrome) during the first year of their lives. There is no definite cause, and most cases of SIDS occurred when babies were sleeping, in their cribs, prams, rocking chairs, and even with mom and dad on their bed. Monitor your baby regularly, and make sure that they aren't wrapped up too warm.

Your baby is at an age when they are able to self-soothe, so you would be able to leave them in their crib when their sleep breaks during the night. They also won't require any nighttime feeding, so your baby would probably sleep through the night. If your baby is still giving you sleep time hassles, then wait to sleep train until they're six months old.

## *What Can I Do to Help My Baby Develop?*

It's time to introduce your baby to solid foods dad! Can you believe it? Your baby is old enough to start eating! This is a big milestone for babies as they are no longer dependent on just milk. Feed your baby rice cereal at first, and then gradually introduce them to pureed vegetables and fruits. Eating healthy is vital for their development. When it comes to physical development, you can help your baby by doing light exercises with them. Continue reading and talking to your baby, as they understand you more now. Take your baby for walks, and allow them to explore. There are also great shows on YouTube that are designed to develop babies' vocabulary and improve their senses.

## *Developmental Problems to Look Out For in Your Five-Month-Old*

- Your baby shows no interest in the surrounding things such as their toys, sounds you make around the house when people talk to them, etc.

- Your baby doesn't take notice of you or show interest when you are engaging with them.

- They aren't making any sounds with their mouth, such as babbling or cooing.

- Their fingers are always tightly clenched in a fist, and they don't open it up.

- You notice that their legs are always bent, and your baby doesn't kick out their legs.

- Whenever you call your baby or make a loud sound, they don't turn to respond to you.

- Your baby seems unhappy all the time, and they are always crabby.

## *Milestones and Changes in Your Baby at Six Months*

Congratulations dad! Your baby has officially reached their half-year mark. Nowadays, parents like to celebrate their babies turning six months old, as they have come so far. They usually celebrate with themed photoshoots and a smash cake session with a cake that has been cut in half to symbolize half a year. Turning six months is a big deal for you and your baby, dad! There are many new developments that take place during this month, and we are going to explore all of them. The more educated you are about the development of your baby, the more involved you can be in helping them develop well. Here's what you need to know about your baby in their sixth month.

### Growth: How Fast is My Baby Growing at Six Months Old?

Your baby is growing at an astounding rate, and they will continue to do so for the next couple of months. The average weight for a sixth-month-old baby should be between 7.2 kg to 7.5 kg, and their height should be around 66-68 cm. I'm sure you must have noticed how much taller and heavier your baby has become, especially when you pick them up from their crib. They would have outgrown much of their clothing by now, which means it's time to change your baby into clothing that is designed to fit six to 12-month-old babies. Their facial features are even more defined, and you can see the resemblance to mom or dad more clearly now. You can now introduce other solids to your baby, such as teething biscuits, boiled vegetables, and soft-boiled pasta and rice. Your baby's diet plays a key role in their development, so ensure that your baby eats well. Please don't discontinue their milk—it's important for them to still feed on either breast or formula milk.

## *Motor Skills: What Can My Baby Do?*

The time has come to be super vigilant with your baby, dad! In addition to rolling over, your baby can also try to push themselves up using their hands and legs when placed on their tummy to play. Most babies aged six months can push themselves up into a crawling position, and they begin moving themselves back and forth while they are still in the same spot. This is a sight to behold as most parents find this hilarious to look at. Their hand control has developed much more as they can now pass toys from one hand to another, and they can reach down and grab their toes. Your baby can even stare at the objects around them and babble to themselves as if they are having a conversation with these objects. At this age, your baby has learned how to play by themselves, which means they can keep themselves entertained while you are busy, but always keep an eye on your baby as anything could happen in a split second.

## *Sleep: How Will My Baby Sleep at Six Months?*

By the time your little one reaches six months of age, they should be sleeping for 9 hours every night, with brief periods of waking up for a feed. This is a good time to sleep train your baby as they are learning to adapt to the world around them. Here's how you should put down your six-month-old baby to sleep.

- When you notice that your baby is feeling sleepy, put them down in the crib. Don't wait for your baby to fall asleep first. This will help them to fall asleep on their own without your help.

- Babies sleep in cycles of 40 mins, and then their sleep breaks. Don't feed your baby thinking that they are hungry. They usually need a few mins to settle back down, so try rubbing their belly gently to help them go back to sleep.

- Set a bedtime routine for your baby. This helps them understand when it's time for bed. If your baby doesn't have a routine, they will trouble you at bedtime.

- Keep the noise to a minimum when you finally get your baby down to sleep. You can try using a white noise machine to keep the atmosphere peaceful.

- Feed your baby before they go to bed. This will give you a peace of mind that they aren't going to wake up for a feed anytime soon. Your baby feeds after every two hours or so, but when they reach six months, their feeds decrease at night.

## *What Can I Do to Help My Baby Develop?*

Your baby is at an age where they love to explore. Give them toys that enhance their senses, such as rattles, prickly plastic balls, teething rings, and toys with bells on them. These toys help develop your baby's sense of touch, sight, and hearing, and the teething rings help them soothe gum irritation when your baby is teething. Here are some activities you can do with your sixth-month-old baby. Read to them (Books with colorful pictures), sing songs, play music, take them for walks, play with toys during bath time, massage them before bed, and do light exercises every morning. Continue what you have been doing for the past four months because it is helping your baby develop each day.

## Developmental Problems to Look Out For in Your Six-Month-Old

Most of the signs on this list have been repeated off the list from five months old. It's important to recognize if your baby has any of these signs, even at six months, so you can take the necessary action to help them.

- Your baby still hasn't been reaching or grabbing their toys, or any other objects placed near them.
- They are having difficulty picking up their heads.
- Your baby hasn't been making any babbling sounds yet.
- When you or your partner walks into the room, your baby cannot recognize you.
- They don't seem interested in their surroundings, such as the curtains flapping in the wind, or the noises coming from the TV.
- Your baby doesn't make eye contact.
- When you call out to your baby, they don't turn or look at you.

## Bonding With Your Baby

It's easy for dads to feel left out when mom is the one who is caring for the baby most of the time. It can be even more difficult for dads when mom is breastfeeding the baby because this is how mothers bond with their babies, and it takes up a lot of time, which means there isn't half as much time left for dads to bond with their babies. With that being said, it is extremely important for fathers to build a connection with their babies. This bond that they build with their dads sets the tone for other relationships they have later on in life. A child who has grown up without their father finds it difficult to open up with people, and because of this, they can't build healthy relationships with others. There are many ways you can bond with your baby, dad, but first, there are a few things you should understand about your baby before you get started.

## *What is Your Baby Learning?*

Your baby will be very interested in colors, shapes, textures, and tastes. Through their senses, they will learn so much about the world around them. When your baby is watching you while you are doing something, they are actually picking up on key behavioral traits and competencies. This is why your baby laughs when you make a funny sound, and why they cry when you use a serious tone of voice. They can understand your emotions as well, which is why babies become restless when mom is upset or stressed. Your baby will use different sounds to communicate their needs with you. People find it incredible how parents know when their babies are hungry, tired, sad, or irritable. Well, it all lies in the way babies communicate with their parents. When you spend time bonding with your baby, you will be able to understand the way they try to communicate with you by the sounds they make.

## *How to Help Your Baby Learn Through Play*

It's sometimes confusing for dads to understand how they can help their baby learn whilst playing, because when you think of the word "play", it points towards fun and games. But when it comes to babies and children, playtime can have a significant impact on their development. One of the key ways you can help your baby learn is to let them explore. All you have to do is create a safe and secure environment for your baby, so that they can play without you worrying about them choking on a small object, or rolling over onto something that could hurt them. Set up mobiles that play music and turn toys around to keep babies engaged in play. Play with your baby, and teach them how to hold their toys. Peekaboo is a great game that parents like to play with their babies because it makes them laugh a lot.

## *What You Should Be Reading to Your Baby*

There are lovely books for babies that you can read for your little one. These books are filled with colorful images and textures that your baby can feel with their hands, such as feathers, stones, fur, and sandpaper. Books like these are very beneficial to the brain development of your baby, so try to get these great texture books for your little one. There are also books that make certain sounds, for example, a book about farm animals that activate sounds when pressed. Reading is an integral part of your child's development, and it should become a stable part of their daily routine even when they are older.

*Connecting With Your Baby*

Dads become easily discouraged when they fail to bond with their babies, just as their partners have. However, they don't stop to think about the ways they can bond with their babies. Below, there is a list of the ways you can bond with your baby.

1. **Become familiar with the five S's**: Knowing how to calm your baby is the first step to bonding. The five S's (swinging, shushing, sucking, swaddling, and side or stomach position) are all key tactics to help calm your baby when they are fussing. Watch mom, and learn a few tips from her about these calming techniques.

2. **Skin-to-skin contact**: Moms aren't the only ones who are lucky enough to bond with their babies via skin-to-skin contact. You can do it too dad! Take off your shirt, and hold your baby close so that they can feel your skin on their face. This will release the hormone called oxytocin which is vital to bond with your baby.

3. **Massage your baby**: This is also a good way of bonding with your child. You can give your baby a massage before bath time or before bedtime, it all depends on which time works best for you and your baby. Babies love a massage, so this is a great way to get into their good books!

*Activities for Dads to Bond With Their Babies*

1. **Change their diapers:** This doesn't have to be a tough task—as most dads avoid it. You can use this

opportunity to talk to your baby and make funny faces whilst changing their diaper.

2. **Blow raspberries**: Babies love it when you blow raspberries on their tummies! This will get your baby laughing instantly.

3. **Dance with your baby:** Dancing is always a happy activity, especially when you have someone to dance with! Put some fun music on and sway to the beat with your baby.

4. **Puppet shows**: This is a fun activity to do with your baby, and it doesn't even cost you a single dollar! Use whatever old socks you have (preferably colorful ones), and stick on some buttons and sequins to create attractive puppets. Set up a puppet show for your baby, and enjoy their reaction.

## *Segue*

This chapter has taught you a lot about how your baby develops during months five and six. You have also learned how to bond with your baby through a variety of activities. The next chapter will focus on educating you about months seven and eight, and it will show you how you can help your partner adjust to this new permanent change in her life.

Chapter 5:

# The Teething Baby and A Seething You

## Adjusting to Life With a Teething Baby!

> *Watching teething babies is like watching over a thermonuclear reactor—it is best done in shifts, by well-rested people.* –Anthony Doerr

In this chapter, you will learn about the developments of your baby during months seven and eight. Your baby will go through a couple of big changes, and they will achieve a few milestones along the way. Life changes after having a baby, and it's important that you and your partner help each other to adjust to this new phase in your lives. This chapter will advise you on how you can help your partner adapt to life after having a baby. By the time you have finished reading this chapter, you will be more confident in yourself as a partner, and as a new father.

## *Milestones and Changes in Your Baby at Seven Months*

Welcome to month seven of your baby's journey! This is the time when your baby will be building on the skills they have already acquired thus far. There are huge milestones that begin to take place in month seven, such as crawling and sitting upright by themselves. However, it's important that you remember every child is different and will develop according to their own pace. Parents must focus on enjoying this journey with their babies because they stay little only for a while. Don't get too caught up in worrying about how your baby is developing, that you completely lose sight of the joy and happiness they bring. Here's what you can expect during month seven of your baby's development.

### *Growth: How Fast is My Baby Growing?*

Your baby is growing very fast dad! I'm sure you must have noticed that by now. They would have picked up a lot of weight, and they would have become taller since the last month. On average, a girl baby should weigh around 7.7 kg, and a boy baby should weigh around 8.4 kg. When you take your baby to the doctor or clinic for their regular checkups, the nurse would check your baby's height and weight. If there is any cause for concern, she would ask you a series of questions to try and understand why your baby has any issues with their weight. Then she will advise you on what you need to do to help your baby reach a healthy, normal weight. Since your baby is now eating solids and drinking milk, it is possible for them to put on more weight than they should. However, it cannot reach an unhealthy level. If your baby is underweight, the nurses might suggest that you change them over to formula (if breastfeeding) so that they can put on weight faster. Your baby will also show signs of teething during month seven. This can be an extremely challenging time for parents as their babies become very restless and crabby because of the teething pains. Teething rings, teething beads, and teething powders are a godsend since they help soothe irritated gums, so make sure that you have these available for your baby.

## *Motor Skills: What Can My Baby Do?*

Month seven holds a few magical milestones for babies as they learn new skills which help them become more independent. One of the first milestones you will notice is your baby being able to sit upright without your help. Their neck muscles would have developed enough by now, which is why they can hold their head up, and balance well whilst sitting. This is still fairly new for your baby, so try not to leave them in a sitting position for too long as it could cause them some discomfort. Another exciting milestone your baby will achieve is crawling! Yes, most babies learn to crawl during month seven, however, there are some who don't achieve this milestone until they are eight or nine months old. This doesn't mean that there is anything wrong with your baby, it just means that they are developing at their own pace. Your baby will also learn new babbling sounds and will add more vowel sounds such as "ohh" and "ahh" to their vocabulary.

## *Sleep: How Will My Baby Sleep at Seven Months?*

As you approach month seven, you will notice that your baby's sleeping schedule is a little more predictable than it was a couple of months ago. They will sleep better at night, but there will be things that cause a disturbance to their sleep, such as teething for example. When babies teeth, they are prone to developing ear infections which could also be interfering with their sleep. If you notice that your baby is crying at night, and unable to stay asleep at night then consider visiting the doctor to rule out any infections. Apart from this, your baby would be falling into a routine that helps them understand when is awake time and when is sleep time. Some babies will sleep throughout the entire night, whilst others still wake up for a feed. These are normal behaviors, so don't get worried about it.

## *What Can I Do to Help My Baby Develop?*

Your baby will enjoy playing games that are repetitive, such as peek-a-boo, and ring around the roses. They will also become drawn to certain music and songs, so it would be great to introduce nursery rhymes for your baby. You can play these nursery rhymes on YouTube, and sing along to these songs in front of your baby. Taking your baby for walks is very beneficial as they are more alert and aware of the world around them. Talk to your baby and tell them about the animals, teach them about the colors, and play with them whenever you can. All of these activities help your baby grow and develop, and it enhances the skills they have already built.

## *Developmental Problems You Should Look Out For in Your Seven-Month-Old*

- Your baby still hasn't made any babbling sounds or vocal sounds yet.

- You notice that they cannot sit upright on their own.

- Your baby doesn't reach for objects or pass them from one hand to another.

- They are unable to push themselves up into a crawling position.

- They don't recognize you, or anyone else that is around them regularly.

- When you try to put your baby in a sitting position, they make their body stiff.

- Your baby still cannot make eye contact.

## *Milestones and Changes in Your Baby at Eight Months*

Welcome to month eight dad! Your baby must be the busiest body ever now that they have found their way around the house. Although they haven't learned to walk just yet, they can still use their hands and legs to get around, especially when they see something they like. This is the stage where your baby will put anything and everything into their mouth, so please be extra careful when you are with your baby. One thing is for sure—your little one isn't the same tiny baby you brought from the hospital all those months ago! They probably have their very own personality by now, and you can tell when they're being stubborn and why. Let's explore the eighth month of your baby's life in more detail below.

### *Growth: How Fast is My Baby Growing?*

By the time your baby reaches eight months, they should weigh between 8.1 kg to 8.9 kg. This is the average weight for their age group, however, there are babies who weigh a little less than 8 kg, and that is fine as long as their weight isn't below 7 kg. Malnutrition occurs when your baby isn't feeding well—whether it is on breastmilk or formula. There could be an underlying issue why your baby isn't gaining any weight, so you need to visit the doctor if your baby isn't feeding or putting on weight properly. Nevertheless, if your baby is within the correct weight and height category, you have nothing to worry about. A couple of teeth would have shown up by now—most probably in the front of your baby's mouth, on the top or bottom gums (sometimes on both). Your baby's head would no longer look larger than the rest of their body, as they have evened out proportionally over the past few weeks.

### *Motor Skills: What Can My Baby Do?*

Your baby has become more advanced and developed both mentally and physically, so they will be moving around a lot, and responding to your gestures. Whenever you talk to your baby, they will be able to respond with babbling as if they understand what you are saying to them. Now that they are crawling, they would have become faster and more familiar with their surroundings, which means that your baby is probably trying to climb up the stairs, open the cabinets in the kitchen, and even chase after the dog to pull their tail! You might have noticed your baby trying to pull themselves up into a standing position with the help of a table or chair. This is how your baby is preparing themselves to start walking, so be careful and always make sure that you are with them whenever they are trying to do this. Your baby will be able to recognize people more easily now, and they probably have a favorite parent! So, how can you tell if your baby likes you? Well, you can't miss that big smile and leaping movements they make whenever they see their favorite parent, that's how you can tell whether your baby likes you.

## *Sleep: How Will My Baby Sleep at Eight Months?*

Finally! The time has come for your baby to sleep without having to wake up at night. By the time your baby reaches eight months of age, they will take around 2–3 naps during the day, and sleep for 10–12 hours at night without waking up for milk. While all this may sound great, there are some parents who still struggle with their baby's sleeping schedule. This has a lot to do with your family dynamic, your environment, and your baby. There have been cases where parents had to deal with sleep disturbances in their babies even after 12 months of age. One of the main reasons for this is a poor sleep routine because of the hectic lifestyle parents have. If you want to make sure that your baby falls into the correct sleeping pattern, you have to put in the work of developing a routine for them to follow from a young age.

## *What Can I Do to Help My Baby Develop?*

This would be a good time to introduce your baby to a walking ring as it can help strengthen their legs and develop their sense of direction. In addition to this, don't forget to massage your baby regularly as their muscles are developing and they can get sore sometimes. Massages also help muscles to become stronger, which helps when your baby is trying to stand up on their own. Ensure that you are giving your baby multivitamins daily to strengthen their immune system and boost growth. Introduce educational toys to your baby, such as building blocks, colorful balls, shapes, and teddy bears. You'd be surprised to see just how much your baby can learn from these different types of toys. Another exciting activity you can do is arrange playdates with other babies. This will help build social skills, and enhance your baby's ability to communicate with others in their own way.

## *Developmental Problems You Should Look Out for in Your Eight-Month-Old*

In addition to the signs mentioned in the previous months, here are a few more you should keep an eye out for.

- You call your baby's name but they don't respond at all.
- Your baby is stuck in a backward crawl and hasn't moved forward yet.
- Your baby hasn't been gaining any weight.
- They have trouble keeping down any solids.
- Your baby isn't sleeping well at night, despite setting a bedtime routine.

## *How to Help Your Partner Embrace Their Role as a New Mom*

After the birth of a baby, a woman goes through many changes mentally, emotionally, and physically. Think about it dad, your partner has just endured nine months of pregnancy, went through a painful delivery, and now she has to take on the role of a mother! Such huge life changes all within a year, without any time to take a breather. Can you imagine how exhausted she must be? This is where you come in dad. Your help and support can make a world of a difference to your partner, but sometimes dads struggle to understand what their partner needs because all the attention is given to the new baby, so there is less communication between mom and dad. If you are having difficulty understanding how you can help your partner, here's some advice for you.

## Communicate With Your Partner

Most relationships end after a baby is born because of a lack of communication between the parents. Mom is too exhausted to talk to dad because she feels he doesn't help, and dad feels neglected because mom spends all her time with the baby, yet no one is willing to voice their concerns! It's important that you break down the barriers that stand in the way of communicating with your partner. Make sure that you set aside time to talk, even if it's just for ten minutes a day. As long as you both are saying what's in your heart, you won't carry any burden that could end your relationship.

## Make Her Feel Loved

Women are often insecure about themselves after pregnancy and birth, so they become a bit closed off from their husbands because they are afraid of what their husbands would say about their physical appearance. No woman deserves to feel insecure about themselves, so the best thing that their husbands could do is make them feel loved and desired. Tell your wife how much you love her, and flirt with her whenever you get a chance. Make her feel like you are still attracted to her, and be patient with her sense of self. It might take a little extra reassuring to help her get her confidence back, but it's worth it. When a woman has confidence in themselves, they can do anything they set their mind to.

## Help Her With the Baby

Believe it or not, but mom is not a superwoman in disguise! She does get tired, and she does need a break from seeing the baby, and cooking and cleaning every day. A woman can actually resent you for watching her do everything while you laze around on the couch. There has been a significant rise in women complaining about the men not helping them around the house, or even with the kids, these days. Men just aren't being as supportive as their partners expect them to. It's your duty, as a father, to help your partner take care of the baby and of the household. It doesn't matter how young or old you may be, the job of a father has to be done. Help her with feeding, or bathing—whatever it is that she needs. That one small task you help her with can make all the difference in her life. She will appreciate you more for helping her when you could have chosen to relax and let her do it all by herself. Your wife will respect you a lot more because you chose to respect her needs.

## *Spend Time With Each Other*

If your wife is secure in the relationship, she will feel more confident as a mother. You can help her feel secure by spending time with her. Life can be hectic after a baby arrives, but that doesn't mean you should neglect one another. Ask a friend or family member to help take care of the baby for a while, so you can spend some quality time with your partner. Tell her what a good job she is doing with your baby, and make her feel appreciated and loved. You can only do this if you have uninterrupted time together. No babies crying in the background, just you and your partner connecting with each other. It's important to put your baby first—yes—but it's also equally important to maintain the bond you have with your partner.

## Self-Care Strategies For New Dads

Don't be surprised, dad. Self-care is important for you as well! As much as mom needs rest, and time to take care of her personal needs, it's also important for dads to take some time for themselves as well. You are the head of your household, which means that there is a lot of pressure on you to make sure that everything is going well with mom and the baby. This requires a lot of time and work on your part dad. Between working and helping out around the house and with the baby, where is the time for you to take care of yourself? Unless you are not well-rested and taken care of, you cannot be everything your family needs you to be. Here's a personal experience of a dad who had severe burnout from a lack of self-care after his baby was born.

### Shaun's Experience as New Dad

"My wife and I had just welcomed our first child into the world a couple of months ago. It was the most exciting day of my life, and I remember being anxious all day long. The first few weeks were amazing! I got to spend time with my baby girl and do all the things parents do when they have a newborn in the home. I must admit, I was getting tired, but I wanted to be a good father so I always put my exhaustion aside so that I could do whatever I could for my baby. My wife had a c-section, and she needed some extra help with going to the bathroom and changing herself. I took care of her while she healed and then went back to work. It was financially strenuous because I was the only one who was employed at the time. My baby needed diapers and formula, so I had to work every day. Fast forward a couple of months, and my baby is now 6 months old."

"Every morning, before I head out to work, I make my little one a bottle and change her diaper. I want to make it easier for mom when she wakes up. When I get back home, I help my wife take care of the baby so that she can get dinner ready for us. Some days I cook, but most of the time my wife cooks because she likes to. Over the weekends, I help my wife out with the chores and I babysit while she attends her part-time classes as she is still studying. Truth be told, we are both trying our best to help one another out, but it does get a bit too hectic for me. I can't remember the last time I went out with the guys, and I no longer have time to visit the barber or to sleep in on my days off. Being a dad is amazing, but it has burned me out. I don't know how to make time for myself, because there are only so many hours in the day! I love my family more than words can say, but I don't think I can help out much longer without breaking down physically and mentally."

### *Six Ways You Can Practice Self-Care*

As you can understand from the above experience—Shaun was at his limit. He couldn't go on giving more of himself because his cup had run dry. Shaun needed time to refuel his energy, and charge his battery so that he could be the best for his family. He didn't want to give them the weakest parts of himself, nor did he want to become frustrated with his partner. Shaun understood that his exhaustion could cost him his marriage, but he didn't know how to find a solution to his problem. This is what happens to many new dads. They want to be superman for their family, but forget to take care of themselves in the process. You have a chance to avoid burnout by learning as much as you can from Shaun's experience. What do you think Shaun could have done to make some time for himself? Would you say that Shaun had dad guilt, and that is why he chose to ignore his own needs every time? Self-care is essential for your overall well-being, dad. You cannot expect your wife to take care of you all the time and tend to your every need. Yes, she can help you, but ultimately, your well-being is your responsibility. Read on further to discover self-care tips that can change your life.

## *Visit the Gym*

Exercise is an important part of maintaining a healthy mind and body. It's also a great way to blow off some steam from a busy day. Consider waking up an hour earlier every morning to visit the gym before you go to work. All you need is an hour a day to keep yourself fit. If you can't make it in the morning, then try to visit the gym before you come home from work. Speak to your partner, and let her know that you are making some positive lifestyle changes. Work out a plan between you two, for babysitting, when either of you has to do some self-care activities. Agree to work together, and help each other find balance in your lives.

## *Make Grooming a Priority*

For guys, grooming is an essential part of their daily or weekly routine. It's important to look neat, especially when you are attending work every day. When you look good, you automatically feel good about yourself, and this boosts your self-confidence. Grooming does take up a lot of time, but it is necessary. Choose a day of the week when you are not too busy—preferably a Friday afternoon or Saturday morning. Make an appointment with the barber so you know that you have to go, despite all the excuses you might come up with. Get your hair cut, and have a shave whilst you're at it. This makes it easier for you and saves you time in the process. Your appearance is important, so make it a priority in your busy life.

### *Eat Healthy*

Being a working dad requires a ton of energy. From the moment you wake up in the morning, till the time you go to bed, your energy will be burning throughout the day so you can get things done. It's vital that you sustain yourself by refueling with healthy food such as fruits and vegetables. The more sugary snacks you consume, the more tired you will feel throughout the day. Clean eating produces a healthy mind and a healthy body that is ready to take on the world. Drink plenty of water, and try to cut down on alcoholic beverages over the week as they can make you feel more drained and tired. If you want to be the best father to your baby, you will have to take care of your health first!

### *Get Some Sleep*

Sleep is a vital aspect of self-care, which many parents don't see much of. During your first year as a parent, you will have to adjust to a new normal which includes less sleep and more coffee! While this might be normal for all parents, it can still have a detrimental impact on your mental and physical durability. The less sleep you get, the higher your chances of experiencing burnout. Ask a friend or family member to help watch the baby while you catch up on some much-needed rest on your day off. Even if it's just two hours of sleep, it can make a world of a difference to your energy levels. Also, try to go to bed earlier at night. As soon as your baby settles down for the night, wrap up whatever it was you were doing, and crawl into bed. You will notice a change in your moods and in your energy level.

### Go Out With Your Friends

Spending time with friends is always a good way to de-stress, especially after you've had a frustrating week. For a family man, it can be difficult to make time for your friends every weekend. You do have a family to take care of, and this can be very time-consuming. Consider setting aside two to three days a month, where you can meet with your friends and have a little time to relax. It's crucial that you don't lose touch with who you were before your baby arrived, and your friends can help you remember the fun guy you really are. Your social life is of great importance, and when you lose touch with it, you become bitter and resentful.

### Spend Time With Your Wife

Tension can also arise when there is conflict between husband and wife. This is common for new parents who struggle to share responsibilities with each other. Either party could feel as if they're doing too much and the other person is doing too little, which then gives rise to disagreements and misunderstandings between a couple. You can disarm the conflict before it gets out of hand by spending time with your partner and talking through issues calmly. The love and support you get from your partner are extremely valuable as they can give you the motivation you need to be a better father. When couples support each other, it helps them succeed in every area of life.

### *Segue*

This chapter has taught you about the development of your baby in months seven and eight. We have also advised you on ways that you can help your partner adjust to their role as a new mother. You have been informed about the importance of self-care for dads, and we have given you great tips to help you practice self-care in your own life. In the next chapter, we take a look at your baby's development from nine months to 12 months of age.

Chapter 6:

# The Cautious Dad Of A Moving Baby

## From Crawling to Walking...and So Much More!

*You keep putting one foot in front of the other, and then one day you look back and you've climbed a mountain.* –Tom Hiddleston

This chapter aims to help you get familiar with the changes your baby will go through during month nine—all the way to month 12. From crawling to walking, from babbling unintelligible words to saying "dada" for the first time—your baby is doing it all! Your journey up to this point has been all about a baby that remained in one place, but now, your baby will have you chasing them around the house!

# *Milestones and Changes in Your Baby During Months Nine to Ten*

Welcome to months nine and ten, dad! This is the most significant time in your baby's development because they go from being an infant to a toddler within a matter of a few weeks. Most parents who work, miss out on these precious moments with their babies because they don't recognize the time frame of these major milestones. You have a chance to prepare yourself for these incredible developments which take place with your baby. So, without further ado, let's get started with exploring how your baby develops over the next two months.

### *Growth: How Fast is My Baby Growing?*

In their ninth month, your baby should weigh around 8.5 kg to 9.3 kg on average. When they reach their tenth month, their weight would increase from around 9.5 kg to 9.7 kg. With all the solid foods they're eating, your baby should be sitting at a good weight for their age. By months nine and 10, your baby would have grown in height as well, and their feet would have also become much longer in size. Continue feeding your baby breastmilk or formula at regular intervals, as they still require the nutrients from the milk to build up a healthy immune system. If you suspect that your baby might be allergic to certain foods, consider getting them checked out by a doctor as soon as possible. Some babies develop an intolerance toward dairy products such as milk, cheese, and yogurt. Others develop allergies to nuts and seafood. As your baby grows, they will eventually have their own likes and dislikes when it comes to food, so pay close attention to what your baby eats happily without fussing.

## *Motor Skills: What Can My Baby Do at Nine/Ten Months*

During months nine to ten, your baby will begin the transition phase from crawling to standing, all on their own! You will notice your baby holding onto the table, or onto your legs for support while they try to stand up. This is an incredible milestone for babies, and most parents are lucky enough to capture these moments on camera. In addition to this, your baby will be very engrossed in the world around them, so keep an eye out because they will be grabbing everything they see. Your baby can now pick up objects using their thumb and their pointer finger, and they can even throw these objects across the room. They will be able to wave at you, and make different hand gestures—most of it they probably learned from you and mom. You will hear a lot more babbling and rambling as if your baby knows exactly what they are saying. They can also recognize items such as their cup or bottles, and they will reach out their hands to grab them.

## *How Will My Baby Sleep at Nine/Ten Months?*

A nine to ten-month-old baby should be getting around 14 hours of sleep a day (including night). Anywhere from 12 to 15 hours is the normal range of sleep a baby should be getting. Now that your baby is quite active during the day, they will nap less. This means that they should be sleeping better at night. A tenth-month-old baby would have one to two naps during the day that are no longer than 60 minutes each. Most of the day, they will be engaged in play and exploring their environment. Every baby is different, and it's understandable that there are different factors that come into play when it comes to how well a baby should be sleeping, but; it is very important that your baby gets no less than 10 hours of sleep a day, especially during month ten. Sleep is crucial for their development, so if a baby doesn't sleep well—they won't be able to develop well. If your baby is having trouble staying asleep at night, visit a doctor for a check-up.

## What Can I Do to Help My Baby Develop?

Since your baby is now at an age where they can pick up on verbal cues, there are many activities you can participate in along with your baby. It's important to choose activities that develop their cognitive abilities and sharpen their hand-eye coordination. Sorting through shapes to join them together is a great activity for developing your baby's skills. Building blocks, practicing drawing with a crayon, and playing with toy animals are activities that will set the foundation for future learning and development. Now that your baby is standing, you can help them take their first few steps by holding their hands and encouraging them to step forward. If your baby hasn't learned how to stand up just yet, give them a little more time. Typically, by the end of the tenth month, your baby would be expressing interest in trying to stand up on their own. With all this physical activity, your baby's growing muscles will become a bit sore. To help ease the pain, and promote development, consider massaging your baby with warm olive oil. All babies love to be massaged, so much so that they manage to sleep through the night after having a good rub. As your baby grows, continue with the reading and singing dad. Play instrumental music, such as the violin and the piano, or you could play Beethoven for your little one whilst they are sleeping. This kind of music is great for the brain development of your baby. Talk to your baby in a positive tone of voice, and teach them different facial expressions. Communication skills are fundamental, so ensure you are teaching your baby how to express themselves clearly.

*Developmental Problems to Look Out For in Your Baby*

- Your baby cannot follow moving objects, even though they are a bit older now.

- They are still having trouble crawling and moving their legs.

- Your baby still doesn't respond when you call their name, or when you make any sounds that should grab their attention.

- Your baby still doesn't smile at you or recognize close family members.

- When you put your baby down, they cannot place their feet firmly on the ground.

## *Milestones and Changes in Your Baby During Months 11 and 12*

Welcome to months 11 and 12, dad! Your baby is almost a year old! Oh, time has flown by so fast. Your baby has become much more independent and playful than before, and they're probably walking all over the house by now. This has been a tiresome journey, no doubt about that, but you have also had some remarkable experiences with your little baby throughout the months. You have seen your baby grow from an infant to a toddler, and there is so much you have learned along the way. Watching your tiny tot grow up is just as difficult as it is exciting. Parents wish that their babies could remain little forever, but we know that we only have a few years to enjoy their childhood before they become teenagers and adults themselves! Nevertheless, let's explore these exciting last two months of your baby's first year.

## Growth: How Fast is My Baby Growing?

Your baby has grown phenomenally throughout these past few months! In months 11 to 12, your baby should weigh around 9.7 kg to 10.4 kg, depending on their gender. Boys tend to put on more weight than girls do, so don't be alarmed if your girl baby is slightly below 10 kg. The growth of your baby is largely contributed to how well they eat solid foods and keep up with their feeds. There will be those tough babies who don't want to eat solids because they prefer to have their milk instead. While it is okay for these babies to continue drinking their milk, it is important for them to eat healthy foods as well. One day, your baby might love pureed butternut with shredded chicken, and the next day they could reject it out of sheer disgust. This confuses parents and makes it all the harder to find food that their baby actually enjoys. All you can do is try different foods, and see which one your baby enjoys most. Try giving your baby multivitamin syrup to boost their appetite if they are rejecting food altogether.

## Motor Skills: What Can My Baby Do?

Your baby has become more communicative and active in their eleventh month. They can say little words like "ball," "hi," "no," "dada," and "mama." They can also understand their emotions a little better, and they will use different tactics to get mom and dad's attention when they don't get their way. Your little pumpkin understands when to throw a tantrum, and you would notice this by their fussing and kicking whenever they see something they want, but can't have. With regard to your baby's physical development, they will definitely be moving around without much hesitation. As they become more confident in themselves, your baby will attempt to climb on top of the tables, chairs, stools—anything they can reach! Please be on the lookout dad, as your baby could potentially fall and hurt themselves.

When your baby reaches 12 months old, they will be known as a toddler. Not forgetting the fact that your baby is now one year old! Most toddlers begin walking by now, even if they take just a few steps forward. Other babies begin walking much earlier—usually around 10 or 11 months. Your baby can clap their hands, dance to the music playing on the radio, and they can hold their own bottles and spoons! Although your baby might not be able to feed themselves just yet, they can drink independently from their bottles at night—with supervision from mom or dad. Their social skills have also developed remarkably by now, as they can play with other babies and share their toys.

## *How Will My Baby Sleep at 11/12 Months?*

Good news dad! Your baby will finally transition into sleeping through the night. At long last, you can get some uninterrupted sleep during the night, however, your baby's day naps would have dropped down to just one long nap a day (two hours). Your baby is more active during the day, with all the moving around they're doing. Sleeping isn't an option for your baby in the daytime, because there's so much more they want to explore. Considering whether you have a sleep routine in place, now might be the time to adjust that routine just a little. Give your baby the freedom to play as long as they want to, and when they feel tired, you can adjust that time of day to nap time. All in all, your baby is doing much better in the sleep department at 11 and 12 months of age. If you are still having trouble with setting a sleep routine for your baby, or if your baby isn't sleeping well throughout the night, book an appointment with the doctor just to make sure everything is okay.

## What Can I Do to Help My Baby Develop?

At this stage in your toddler's development, physical love and affection is very important. You can show your baby how much you love them through hugging, giving kisses, cuddling, and cheering them on with words of encouragement such as "Good job." The warmth you show your toddler through your acts of love, grooms them to be loving and expressive with their emotions from a young age. As far as toys are concerned, switch them up for regular household items such as pegs and plastic containers. You'd be surprised how much toddlers love playing with these things. Have story time, sing nursery rhymes, and play exciting games like hide and seek. Encourage your baby to play well with others, and take them out of the house so that they can meet other toddlers and be social. Allow your toddler to try and feed themselves with a spoon. You can make dinner time fun by making a few easy finger foods that your toddler will be able to pick up and put into their mouth. Always keep an eye on your toddler whilst they are eating, and ensure that all foods are cut up into little portions to avoid a choking situation.

## Developmental Problems to Look Out For in Your Baby

- Your toddler doesn't respond to simple instructions.
- You can't get your toddler to make eye contact with you.
- You notice that they can't see or hear clearly.

- They can't wave or point their fingers at something they are interested in.

- They aren't using any single words as yet, such as "dada" or "mama."

- You have trouble getting your toddler to stand up.

- Your toddler doesn't react whenever they see you or your partner.

## *Emotional, Social, and Mental Development of Babies and What You Can Do as a Dad*

Parents sometimes become fixated on the physical development of their babies, and they completely ignore the emotional side which is also developing along with the physical side. Your baby's emotional development is just as vital as their physical development. Just because you can't see their emotions, it doesn't mean that they aren't growing and changing as well. Mothers and fathers have the responsibility to ensure that their babies are being loved and cared for properly, as this can have a huge impact on the mental and emotional well-being of the child. Let's take a look at the emotional developments your baby goes through between eight and 12 months of age.

### *Emotional and Social Development of Your Baby From Eight to 12 Months*

Parents will notice two different sides to their baby during this stage in their development. On one hand, your baby would seem loving, outgoing, and playful with you, and on the other hand, they would also be clingy, anxious, and irritable at times. Some parents find it difficult to juggle all of these emotions, especially when their babies keep changing their mood every ten minutes! This is completely normal dad, so don't fear when people tell you that you might be doing something wrong because you're not. Your baby is newly discovering their feelings, so it's okay for them to be a little mixed up at times. One of the first emotional milestones your baby will experience is feelings of anxiety when they are around people they don't know. You will notice how upset your baby becomes the minute an unfamiliar face comes around them.

Separation anxiety is another emotional milestone your baby will achieve. At about eight or nine months, you will recognize signs of separation anxiety that make themselves known in your baby. They will become clingier, and every time you try to leave the room—even for a little while—they will suddenly burst out crying. Also, whenever you try to leave your baby with the nanny or with another family member, they will not be happy about it and they will express themselves by crying and moaning. Mothers who breastfeed can experience separation anxiety much earlier on with their babies, and it can be more severe. As your baby grows, their separation anxiety will die down eventually as long as you are handling it the right way, with the right techniques.

### The Role of Dads in the Social and Emotional Development of Babies

Your role as a father holds much importance in your child's life. Most fathers have no clue as to how much they could actually impact the emotional and social development of their children because they believe that it's the mothers who have all the influence when it comes to being emotional and in touch with their feelings. Dad, your influence is greater than moms when it comes to the emotional side of things. Let's take a look at the different ways you can impact the development of your baby emotionally and socially.

## *Boosts Intelligence*

A present father who is actively involved in a child's life, especially during the first year, helps to build their child's emotional intelligence by being involved in their development. Studies have shown that children who have active fathers score much higher on cognitive assessments because they are confident in their curiosity to explore the world around them. This promotes verbal skills development, as well as mental concentration in children (Child Crisis AZ, 2017). To put it in simple terms—a dad who is present raises children that are emotionally and mentally intelligent.

## *Increases Confidence*

Dads also play a key role in helping their children gain confidence in themselves. When your child is going through a difficult time with their emotions, you can help them build a healthy self-esteem by encouraging them and cheering them on in their moments of weakness. Children who have supportive fathers are more likely to have a healthy sense of self-confidence because they know that they have the love and guidance of their dad. If you had to observe a child who grew up without a father, or a child who grew up with a father who never showed them love, you would instantly pick up on their lack of confidence in themselves. This is because they feel unworthy or unlovable because of the absence of a father's love.

## *Role Model*

For male children, having a father as a role model is one of the most important aspects of their emotional development. A boy child needs someone to look up to, so the first person they will turn to is their fathers, not their mothers. You can be a good role model for your child by showing them love, supporting them in their challenging times, teaching them right from wrong, and taking care of them the way a father is supposed to. Remember, your child is watching your every move from a young age, and they will pick up on everything you say and do. If you use kind words around your baby, then they will grow up speaking kind words to others. But if you use vulgar words in front of your baby, then their first words would be vulgar as well. Carry yourself in the same way you would like your child to be when they grow up.

## *Segue*

In this chapter you have learned everything there is to know about months nine to twelve of your baby's development.
Whatever questions you may have had about the development of your baby, have been answered in great detail within this chapter. There are a few appendices that follow down below. There is a feeding chart that serves as a guide to help you plan your own for your baby, and there is a vaccination chart that gives you the correct age and vaccines required so you can make a note of these important vaccine schedules.

# Appendices

## Baby Feeding Chart

| Food | 4-6 Months | 6-8 Months | 8-10 months | 10-12 Months |
|---|---|---|---|---|
| **Cereals, Grains, and Pulses** | Rice cereal<br>Oats<br>Maize porridge | Rice<br>Lentils<br>Beans- Pinto, Black, Red<br>Oats | Pasta<br>Rice<br>Oats<br>Lentils/Beans | All Cereals, grains, and pulses |
| **Vegetables** | Pureed butternut<br>Sweet potatoes<br>Peas, and squash | Green Beans<br>Parsnips<br>Squash<br>Peas<br>Butternut | Mushrooms<br>Broccoli<br>Onions<br>Egg plant | Cucumbers<br>Corn<br>Spinach<br>Asparagus |
| **Fruits** | Pureed Banana, apples, | Mangoes<br>Pumpkin | Grapes<br>Kiwi<br>Blueberries | All these fruits<br>Citrus |

|  |  |  |  |  |
|---|---|---|---|---|
|  | avocados, carrots, and pears | Prunes<br>Apricots | Raspberries<br>Strawberries<br>Plums | fruits such as oranges and nectarines |
| **Dairy** | Strictly Breastmilk or Formula | Breastmilk<br>Formula<br>Whole Milk Yogurt **(keep an eye out for allergies)** | Cheese<br>Yogurt<br>Milkshakes<br>Breastmilk<br>Formula | Breastmilk<br>Formula<br>All dairy products |
| **Proteins** | Breastmilk<br>Formula | Shredded Chicken<br>Tofu | Soft Beef<br>Chicken<br>Fish **(keep an eye out for allergies)** | Eggs<br>Meat cooked well done<br>Soya products<br>Legumes |

## Vaccination Chart

| Age | Vaccines Scheduled |
|---|---|
| Birth | • **BCG**-Bacille Calmette-Geurin<br>• **OPV(0)**-Oral Polio Vaccine |

| | |
|---|---|
| 6 weeks | - **OPV(1)**<br>- **RV (1)**-Rotavirus vaccine<br>- **DTaP-IPV-Hib-HepB (1)**- Diphtheria+Tetanus+Acellular Pertussis vaccine+Inactive+Polio vaccine+Haemophilus Influenzae type B vaccine+Hepatitis B vaccine (all combined)<br>- **PCV (1)**-Pneumococcal Conjugate vaccine |
| 10 weeks | - **DTaP-IPV-Hib-HepB (2)** |
| 14 weeks | - **RV(2)**<br>- **DTaP-IPV-Hib-HepB (3)**<br>- **PCV(2)** |
| 6 months | - Measles vaccine (1) |
| 9 months | - **PCV(3)** |
| 12 months | - Measles vaccine (2) |
| 18 months | - **DTaP-IPV-Hib-HepB (4)** |

| 6 years | • (**Td**)-Tetanus and reduced-strength Diphtheria vaccine |
|---|---|
| 9 years | • **HPV**-Human Papillomavirus vaccine (**1 and 2** given 6 months apart) |

## Baby Milestone Chart (1-12 months)

| 1st Month | 2nd Month | 3rd Month |
|---|---|---|
| • Can lift their head when placed on their tummy<br>• Has a firm grip<br>• Can follow movement with their eyes | • Can make gurgling sounds<br>• Will bring their hands up to their mouth<br>• Can smile while they're awake and in their sleep | • Can recognize mom and dads face and their scent<br>• Can do push ups during tummy time<br>• Reacts to loud noises |

| 4th Month | 5th Month | 6th Month |
|---|---|---|
| • Can roll over onto their tummy<br>• Engages in | • Will start to babble and make cooing | • Can laugh and giggle<br>• Will begin to sit upright |

|  |  |  |
|---|---|---|
| play with mom and dad<br>• Teething might start | sounds<br>• Can pass objects from one hand to another<br>• Start eating solids | with your help<br>• Can recognize familiar faces |

| 7th Month | 8th Month | 9th Month |
|---|---|---|
| • Can sit upright without any help<br>• Will begin to form crawling positions<br>• Can play independently | • Can clap their hands<br>• Will lean over to pick up objects<br>• Can crawl well | • Will respond when you call their name<br>• Can mimic the movements of mom and dad<br>• Will try to stand up by holding onto objects |

| 10th Month | 11th Month | 12th Month |
|---|---|---|
| • Can imitate words such as "dada" and "mama"<br>• Can stack toys or building blocks | • Will begin to stand upright without support<br>• Can say "mama" and | • Might start walking by taking their first few steps<br>• Can wave their hands and point to objects |

| | | |
|---|---|---|
| • Can crawl faster without hesitation | "dada" clearly<br>• Will respond when their name is called | • Improved hand-eye coordination |

# Conclusion

Congratulations dad! You are now 100% ready to face the first 12 months with your new baby. This wonderful journey you have embarked on is filled with many precious moments which you will share with your little one. In chapter one, you learned about the first 24 hours of your baby's life. The important points emphasized in this chapter were about the events that take place from the moment your baby is born; birth defects to look out for; what goes on in the NICU; how to support your partner with postpartum depression; and how to take care of your newborn. It might seem like a lot of information to take in; but when you see it happening, it will jog your memory and bring back everything you have learned.

From chapter two through chapter six, you were educated on the developments that take place with your baby from months one to 12. Within each chapter, you also learned about your roles and responsibilities as a working dad; how to balance your work life and home life; ways you can bond with your baby; how to help your partner step into their new role as a mom; self-care tips to prevent burnout; and how your role as a father impact your baby's social and emotional development. These are all major aspects of your life as a new dad, so try your best to follow the guidance provided to you under each of these sections. There are millions of first-time dads who have many regrets after spending the initial 12 months as a learn-as-you-go experience. They wish they had sought advice or help earlier on so they could have done things differently with their babies. These dads knew nothing about bonding with their babies, how their babies develop, or what type of vaccines their babies needed!

You have a headstart dad! This guide has equipped you with all the information you need to be a great father to your baby. There's only one thing that can stop you from being the best dad you can be—your own fear. Use the knowledge you have accumulated over the course of reading this book and compile a weapon against your fears. Defeat each fear by putting into practice all that you have learned so far. There's a lot resting on your shoulders, dad. Your partner is depending on you to be her support system to get her through her healing, and to hold her hand as she embraces her new role as a mother. Your baby is dependent on you to provide them with all they need emotionally and physically.

This journey of fatherhood is an incredible experience that will define who you are in many ways. The legacy you leave behind will be evident through the children you raise. Every decision you make as a dad will be seen in the lives of your children, so make sure that you are wise in everything you do. Wade Boggs rightly said, "Anyone can be a father, but it takes someone special to be a dad." Are you ready to be a dad?

You found this book when you were in need of help and support as a new father, now you are confident in your role as a dad. Please leave a review by scanning the QR code in the beginning of this book so that this book can reach other parents who are in need of support and guidance on their journeys as well. Thank you!

# References

A quote from Jared Padalecki that every parent can relate too | How are you feeling, Jared Padalecki, Quotes. (n.d.). *Pinterest.* https://www.pinterest.ie/pin/a-quote-from-jared-padalecki-that-every-parent-can-relate-too--851321135795911794/

Aug 10, J. B., & 2021. (2021, August 10). 11 Ways Dads Can Practice Self Care and Why They Should (Yes, Even You!). *The Dad.* https://www.thedad.com/dads-self-care/

Baby teeth, Teeth quotes, Funny baby quotes. (n.d.). *Pinterest.* https://za.pinterest.com/pin/215258057166000192/

Bedortha, A. (2020, February 5). Modern Fatherhood: Balancing Work-Family Life. *Parenting Now.* https://parentingnow.org/modern-fatherhood-balancing-work-family-life/

Ben-Joseph, E. P. (2018, June). The First Day of Life (for Parents) - Nemours KidsHealth. *Kidshealth.org.* https://kidshealth.org/en/parents/first-day.html

Centers for Disease Control and Prevention. (2021). Birth-18 years immunization schedule. Centers for Disease Control and Prevention; *CDC.* https://www.cdc.gov/vaccines/schedules/hcp/imz/child-adolescent.html

Child Crisis AZ. (2017, June 5). 5 Important Ways Fathers Impact Child Development - Child Crisis. *Child Crisis.* https://childcrisisaz.org/5-major-ways-fathers-impact-child-development/

Davies, I. (2021, January 19). 88 Baby First Steps Quotes - Celebrating This Incredible Milestone. *Find Your Mom Tribe.* https://findyourmomtribe.com/baby-first-steps-quotes/

Fun Bonding Activities for Dads and Babies. (n.d.). Child Development Institute. February 13, 2023, https://childdevelopmentinfo.com/how-to-be-a-parent/fun-bonding-activities-for-dads-and-babies/

Horsager-Boehrer, R. (2021, August 17). 1 in 10 dads experience postpartum depression, anxiety: How to spot the signs | Your Pregnancy Matters | UT Southwestern Medical Center. *Utswmed.org.* https://utswmed.org/medblog/paternal-postpartum-depression/

McElroy, M. (2014, January 6). Babbling babies – responding to one-on-one "baby talk" – master more words. *UW News.* https://www.washington.edu/news/2014/01/06/babbling-babies-responding-to-one-on-one-baby-talk-master-more-words/

Pin by Maayan Orit on Shlomo | Milestone chart, Baby development, Baby milestone chart. (n.d.). *Pinterest.* February 16, 2023, https://za.pinterest.com/pin/146859637821500190/

Rose Kennedy Quotes. (n.d.). *BrainyQuote*. January 20, 2023, https://www.brainyquote.com/authors/rose-kennedy-quotes

The Children's Hospital of Philadelphia. (2019, January 3). How to Cope When Your Unborn Baby is Diagnosed with a Birth Defect | Children's Hospital of Philadelphia. *Chop.edu*. https://www.chop.edu/news/how-cope-when-your-unborn-baby-diagnosed-birth-defect

Uplifting Quotes About Fatherhood. (2019, June 12). *Lingokids - the PlaylearningTM App in English*. https://lingokids.com/blog/posts/dad-quotes

Watson, S. (2009, October 20). Baby Development: Your 1-month-old. WebMD; *WebMD*. https://www.webmd.com/parenting/baby/baby-development-1-month

Winder, K. (2006, March 20). How Dads Can Help New Mothers After Baby's Birth. *BellyBelly*. https://www.bellybelly.com.au/men/how-you-can-help-mum-after-your-babys-birth/

www.ingramcontent.com/pod-product-compliance
Lightning Source LLC
Chambersburg PA
CBHW070951080526
44587CB00015B/2262